Connect With The Divine You

For Health, Healing & Happiness

Dear Hannah,

Sending you so much love, Courage
& Strength to walk you path to
healing — it is possible to fully heal
M.S. (+ anything else). If you ever
want to talk, call or text 928-606-0976
or tanya@tanyapenny.com.

T.P. :)

Tanya Penny

Manor House

Library and Archives Data:
Title: Connect With The Divine You / Tanya Penny
Softcover ISBN: 978-1-988058-34-4 List: $19.95
Hardcover ISBN: 978-1-988058-35-1 List: $39.95
1. Self-actualization (Psychology) in women
2. Self-control   3. Title
SEL021000   SEL031000   BF637.S4S426 2018
Non-Fiction: Self-Help, self-healing, health, happiness
Release: Feb. 7/2018   Page Count: 144   Trim: 6x9"
Publisher/Imprint: Manor House Publishing Inc.
Contact: 905-648-2193 mbdavie@manor-house.biz
Photos of author (front and back cover): Janna Waldinger
Cover design-layout: Amy Greensky / Michael Davie

This book is for all the brave souls who are on a healing journey. Whether you have anxiety, depression, weight, an autoimmune disorder, other chronic illness, past trauma, or another life breakdown- money, relationships, career, it takes tremendous courage and perseverance. Don't ever give up, you can do it.

Acknowledgements

A big heartfelt THANK YOU to everyone who has been on my healing journey with me thus far, and to those who continue to walk this crazy path with me today, but especially: My parents (Steve & Cheryl), Josh, Fran, Suzanne, Dr. J, Calla, Games, Rebecca, Will, Jennifer, my clients, Susan Crossman for editing assistance, Michael Davie and Manor House for publishing my book, Janna Waldinger for author photos, Amy Greensky for cover design work – and many, many more — you know who you are. ☺

Table of Contents

Praise for *Connect With The Divine You*:

"**Tanya Penny** has written a powerful book about connecting with who we are and who we are truly on the planet to be. Her writing is clear, concise and focused on providing the insights and practical tools that help clear away the clutter of the past and allow us to move forward into a more promising future. With compassion and care, she lays out a path that anyone can follow and everyone can leverage."

Susan Crossman, Best-selling author, *Passages to Epiphany*

'**Tanya Penny** is a relentless seeker of deeper truth, and I am blessed to witness some of her vulnerable journey. Her book touched my heart and I know they will give so many hope when things may seem hopeless. Thanks for having the courage to share your journey in such a heartfelt yet practical way, Tanya.'

Jennifer Hough, Best-selling Author/Speaker/Seer

"I've watched Tanya's physical, spiritual connection unveil in her life over the years. There is no better teacher than someone who has walked the healing path and is now on the other side. Her journey has taken her from disease to health and happiness. If you have disease or dysfunction this book is a tool to bring you to a state of connection with your inner ability to heal, be healthy and prosper in all areas of your life."

Dr. Jennifer Anacker, Anacker Chiropractic

"... Tanya Penny can absolutely guide you on your personal journey to self love and connecting to the Divine You. She lays out step-by-step how to face yourself and open your heart to you, the Divine You, the most important thing you will ever do in this life. Without self-love and acceptance, suffering will be a way of life. Tanya has provided the process and tools to end your suffering. This is not just another feel good book, it's a self-healing guide that anyone can follow."

- **Bonnie Serratore**, Author, **The Way Back Home**

Foreword

Many of us become disconnected from our true Self for many reasons while growing up.

Over time, this disconnection can cause all sorts of health problems in our minds and bodies, as well as breakdowns in other important life areas: our relationships, our finances, our careers and life purpose.

In this book, **Tanya Penny** teaches you a mind-body-spirit process that will support you to re-connect with and accept all parts of yourself: your desires, your breath, your body, your emotions, your beliefs, and your "Something Bigger."

Tanya Penny's Therapeutic Meditation Process (TMP), combined with her mind-body-spirit healing philosophy, reflection and journaling exercises, guided meditation practices, plus other tools and inspired actions, will all support you to listen to your body, release toxic emotions, shift limiting beliefs, connect with your inner guidance, and ultimately walk the path to healing yourself.

If you desire enhanced health, happiness and the opportunity to live the passionate, abundant life of your dreams, this book and the process Tanya teaches will support you to your enjoyment of it.

Introduction

It feels surreal to be writing this book about self-connection and also using the word "divine." If you had told me 20 years ago that I would be writing a book with this theme, I would have laughed my ass off and said "Yeah — when Hell freezes over!"

I did everything possible to NOT connect with myself. I escaped being with myself by overeating, drinking, taking drugs, sleeping, working and staying very "busy."

When I turned 18, my parents stopped forcing me to go to church, which allowed me to cut off all connection to anything bigger than me. The word "divine," and anything else that even slightly implied that God or religion was somehow involved in my world, sent me running the other way.

So how did I get to today, when I find myself authoring a book about self-connection and the divine —two "forbidden" subjects? Good question. In a nutshell, I was diagnosed with the chronic illness, Multiple Sclerosis (MS), in 2004. Before that, I had struggled with anxiety, depression, eating disorders, alcohol abuse and weight problems.

The MS diagnosis was the cherry on the top of my shit sundae. It was also the answer to many of my prayers, leading me to happiness, peace, and the discovery of my purpose. My "journey of the wounded healer" had begun.

Like most people who are diagnosed with a chronic and progressive illness, I first looked to western medicine to help me manage my symptoms and, ultimately — hopefully — find a cure.

At the time, my neurologist told me that I had a 30% chance of slowing down the progression of the disease if I followed western medical practices, but that there was no cure. To this day, doctors still say there is no cure. Not true in my book. ☺

For three years, I walked the western medicine path. I gave myself treatment shots every other day, which I dreaded. The medicine that was only 30% effective in slowing down the progression of my disease gave me flu-like symptoms for 24 hours every time I injected it, and it often kept me from getting out of bed.

Year after year I would get better for a while, and then have yet another relapse, and my symptoms worsened. Multiple Sclerosis is a disease that can affect everyone differently.

At first, I had trouble speaking and finding words. Shortly after diagnosis, I lost vision in my right eye, and experienced overwhelming fatigue. I then experienced weakness and numbness on the right side of my body, similar to what happens with a stroke, and some days that affected my left side, too. On top of it all, I struggled with pain, insomnia, depression, and anxiety.

Before all of this, I was someone who had worked 50 hours a week, and ran daily. I had even run a marathon. Now there were days when I could barely work four hours in a day, or walk 50 feet before needing to rest. I felt hopeless and defeated. I hated my body and my life.

My Turning Point

My turning point came in September 2007, after yet another MS relapse.

As usual, I went to the emergency room and had the infusion of prednisone that had been recommended by my doctor as a means of decreasing the damage to my brain and body. Prednisone made me crazy — mentally, physically and emotionally. My nerves would be on fire for weeks after those shots. I couldn't tolerate noise and I couldn't sleep. In fact, it was impossible for anyone to be around me. I tended to isolate myself as much as possible until the effects wore off.

This particular time, a friend offered me the use of her cabin in northern Idaho as a "recovery hideout." This was one of my favorite places because nature and the mountains were very soothing to me, especially when I was feeling bat-shit crazy.

One morning, I went to inject the dreaded shot of MS medicine into my stomach and something stopped me. It wasn't the multiple scars on my body from the prior shots, or my fear of the pain the shots caused.

I actually heard a voice that said, "Stop. There is another way. Put the syringe and medicine down for good." I never gave myself that shot of medicine, or any western medicine for MS again.

I went home a few days later and told my husband and my doctor that I was not giving myself the shots anymore. This did not go over well, to say the least. They begged me to change my mind, but I could not.

It was not easy, but I knew I had to listen to that voice, whatever or whoever it was. The journey of connecting with my divine self to heal my mind, body, and spirit had begun.

I started searching and trying many, many different alternative treatments: nutrition, acupuncture, chiropractic care, bodywork, yoga, meditation, and more.

I started studying mind-body healing philosophy and dug out the book, *You Can Heal Your Body* by Louise Hay that I had purchased 10 years before. I started reading it. I completely immersed myself in alternative healing and started feeling better, little by little.

Fast forward to today, almost 12 years after my initial diagnosis. I no longer experience any of the MS symptoms that I mentioned earlier. In fact, that's been the case for more than six years. I run and hike daily. I can actually hike 10 miles in one day carrying a 30-pound backpack. I run my own business, working as much as I choose. I have gotten my vibrant body and passionate life back!

I believe that the day I was diagnosed with MS was the day my prayers were answered. It has not been an easy journey. But I know it all happened for a good and necessary reason: to connect with my divine self again and to support you to do it, too.

Whether you struggle with anxiety, depression, weight, or chronic illness, this book can help you… if you keep an open heart and mind.

I can't promise recovery or remission. But I can promise support and a blueprint for well-being that has made a huge difference in my life and in the lives of my clients.

In these chapters, I will be sharing with you my personal experiences and providing tools to connect with the divine you. As I teach all my clients (and as I needed to learn myself), you are your own guru and you have all your own answers.

I am only here as your guide, to share with you what I have learned on my journey to healing mind, body, and spirit

I never tell anyone to go off western medicine. I believe that some of us need both and some of us do not — we all have a different path.

I also believe that the things we need in order to heal are brought to us in divine time, when we are ready. So, if you have this book in your hands, I am guessing you are ready, and that there is something in these pages you will find necessary to your healing journey.

As you are reading this book, and applying the keys, tools and concepts I am sharing, remember to always check in with yourself and ask what is right and true for you. Take what you like and what resonates with you, then leave the rest.

I am truly honored and excited to be on this journey with you, and to be able to share what has supported me and hundreds of others to heal, to have a vibrant body, and to live an abundant life of freedom.

Sending you love, hope and courage to walk your healing path,

Tanya Penny ☺

Chapter 1: The Truth About Self-Connection

Disconnection from Self is the number one cause of illness, mind and body. – Tanya Penny

I believe that disconnection from Self is the Number One cause and driver of illness and disease, and that it's responsible for anxiety, depression, weight issues, pain and any other negative symptom or "feeling" in the body.

Dis-ease with the self and spirit creates Disease mentally, physically and emotionally.

Reconnecting with, accepting, being and expressing your true Self — your desires, body, feelings, emotions and thoughts — are all essential to heal your body and feel peaceful and happy.

What Causes Disconnection?

Through my own experience, I've determined that there are five main reasons why we become disconnected from our Self.

1. **You were corrected, criticized or rejected:** I grew up with a very critical and perfectionistic dad. I was often corrected and/or criticized for what I did, or what I didn't do "right." I also saw him criticize my mom and others, too. He wasn't trying to be "mean." He was just following a pattern that had been set for him when he himself had been a child. When we grow up being corrected or criticized for our desires, body, thoughts, emotions, actions, etc., we begin to shut down. When we get to school, we try to fit in and be liked. Some of us are even teased for who we are. So, we slowly learn to turn off who we are and try to speak and act in ways that will please others, so we won't be criticized or rejected. Not only did I get the criticism at home, but I got picked on by boys at school. Years and years later I found out it was because they liked me, but when it was happening, I thought it was because there was something wrong with me. That all results in the belief that we are not good enough or "likeable" when we are being our true self, so we stop wanting to be that person.

2. **You didn't see your parent(s) connect with themselves:** We often model, or do what we see, while growing up. I saw both my parents do a lot of escaping from themselves — excessive TV watching plus overdrinking, eating, and *doing* (they were constantly busy). I also saw my mom doing things just to please others. Sometimes this meant that she left little time to do what she truly desired. She also stopped

18

doing some things because she didn't want to be criticized by my dad. I saw her try to communicate her feelings, emotions and desires to my dad, only to be yelled at and criticized. Eventually, she stopped. I, of course, started to model these same behaviors in my daily life and relationships, too. As I got older, I fell into overeating and then drinking to suppress my unexpressed emotions, and I found myself trying to please the men that I was with, even if it meant doing things I didn't want to do. I put up with a lot of unacceptable behavior and went against myself in a lot of ways. When we don't have healthy self-connection models, this is what we do.

3. **You experienced abuse.** When we have an experience of abuse — verbal, physical, sexual or neglect — we believe that something must be wrong with us, that we are bad, etc., and we begin to dislike and even hate ourselves. We also feel shame, and on some level even blame ourselves for it happening in the first place. So, why on Earth would we want to connect with ourselves when we believe we are bad or awful? I was sexually abused by some male cousins and then, years later, at the age of 15, I was date-raped by a boy I had just started dating. I told no one about any of these experiences until I was in my twenties because I was ashamed and scared, and I also blamed myself. I continued to date that boy and have sex with him because he threatened me. I hated myself and my body. To disconnect and suppress the way I felt, I drank

too much and developed eating disorders. I also pushed myself mentally and physically in school, and then at work, both to prove that I was worthwhile and good, and to stay busy so I could then ignore my negative inner voice.

4. **You experienced one or more traumas.** Besides abuse, many of us experience one or more traumas in our life. Many of us don't even realize this because it might have been something "small" or maybe someone told you "it" was no big deal, so you brushed it off. You might have been teased or bullied in school. Perhaps, you were in an accident. Maybe you were diagnosed with a chronic illness. There is an underlying belief that bad things happen to bad people. You must have deserved it, or even caused this bad thing to happen. These traumas often affect us emotionally, mentally and physically, leaving us feeling inferior. When we feel bad or inferior, we often want to disconnect from or get rid of these parts of ourselves.

5. **You are too busy, and don't make enough space or down-time to connect.** Most of us learn from our culture, society, and family that staying busy, constantly doing, and working hard is the way to survive, be worthwhile, and live a successful life. This starts at a very young age. Kids go to school all day, participate in an after-school activity, do homework, squeeze in a little T.V. or computer time and then finally drop into bed. We then continue this pattern into adulthood. We over-work ourselves in our job

or career so we can get promoted, make more money and ensure job security. We over-do and stay constantly busy in our personal lives with chores, friends, family, etc. Many of us do things just to please others, or because we think we should or that we have to. When we don't make enough space and time in our schedule to rest, or to be or do what we like, then we slowly become more and more disconnected from who we really are. We don't even take the time to reflect on what we desire, or explore who we really are. This causes a great deal of stress that we try to escape feeling, and we stuff ourselves with food, alcohol, drugs, TV or computer use, shopping, etc.

Tips, Tools and Inspired Actions:

Remember that awareness is the key to changing anything in your life. Let go of any judgement and reflect with compassion and curiosity on the following:

1. Rate, on a scale of 1-10, how connected you feel to your Self at this moment. 0 = not at all. 10 = completely, deeply connected.

2. Reflect on the following questions:

- Which of the above reasons led you to disconnect from your Self initially?

- Why do you think you continue to be disconnected from your Self today?

3. Have you noticed any judgement, blame or shame come up with this reflection? If yes, know that this is normal. Take a moment and write down what the voice in your head or inner critic is saying. We will work with these judgements and beliefs as we move through the book.

The Truth About Self-Connection:

A Client Connection

Joe's Story

Joe was having some neurological-related symptoms, and he knew I had had some success in supporting people with Multiple Sclerosis. He was experiencing vision and hearing loss, and some facial paralysis. He tended to be super-critical and was easily frustrated with himself and others.

Why He Came to See Me

Joe and I had worked together years earlier at a rehabilitation hospital where I had been an occupational therapist. Years after our paths had taken us in different directions, I received an email from Joe asking if we could talk. He wanted to reduce his anxiety, enjoy more loving, fun and respectful relationships with others, and make more time to connect with himself daily.

Joe was aware that he had a very harsh inner critic that relentlessly beat him up for what he didn't do or do "right," especially at work. He also knew that he pushed himself too hard, and tended to take on too much. He wasn't feeling fully respected or heard in his marriage, and he felt judged. He judged his wife's actions as well, and he was often overwhelmed by his responsibility for his family, which included two young girls. Joe had previously had many close friendships, but since becoming a father and husband, he had less and less time, and he was now feeling lonely and disconnected from himself and others.

How We Worked Together

Joe had spent a fortune on Western medicine already, and his time and finances were limited. We decided that the best way for us to work together was to start with one private session by phone to give him insight into the root causes of the breakdown in his health and life. This would also give us an opportunity to come up with some inspired actions he could take to start healing the patterns that had led to his dis-ease.

He started by listening to my "Connecting with The Divine You" (Therapeutic Meditation Process) audio lessons, and using my guided Therapeutic Meditation Practices, supplemented by a daily "reflect and write" journaling practice. We then had a follow-up phone session a month later to tweak the inspired actions and make more recommendations.

We decided that Joe would benefit from participating in my Vibrant Body & Abundant Life Mastery group program to address the 10 Keys to Health. This would provide him the wisdom, support, and tools he needed to heal his relationship issues, create more work-life balance, and help him to fully accept and love himself, all of which would together contribute to healing his health symptoms.

The Issue at the Heart of the Matter

Joe agreed that perfection played a big role in most of his issues, along with his tendency to pretend to be Superman (over-doing things) and trying to please everyone else. He took on too much and pushed himself too hard at work to prove that he was "good enough."

Then, when he couldn't keep up or do everything perfectly, he beat himself up for it. The same thing happened at home. Joe tried to be the perfect husband and father in order to please his wife and children — at the expense of his own needs and desires. When he couldn't master everything all at the same time, his inner critic let him have it, again.

Trying to be a perfect "Superman" and please everyone else took a lot of time and energy, leaving very little time for Joe to connect with himself or have fun. Plus, the constant beating up on himself caused him to disconnect from himself even more. He was trapped in a vicious cycle.

Over the course of our time together, I asked Joe to carve out time to connect with himself daily through reflecting and writing five-to-ten minutes a day, and using a guided therapeutic meditation practice in the morning and again at bedtime as he fell asleep. He used these tools to also accept himself, to plant the seeds for what he desired in his life, to feel and release emotions of guilt and blame, to shift the limiting beliefs that were causing him to get stuck in the patterns of pushing himself too hard, working too much, trying to please others, and looking at what, in his past, might have contributed to these beliefs/patterns.

Joe discovered many things through using the self-connection process daily. In reflecting on his past, he saw how being an only child put a lot of pressure on him to "do it all" and be perfect.

Even though Joe knew his mother loved him very much, she tended to be needy and over-bearing, wanting a lot of his time and attention. She was also a people-pleaser, often tending to other people's needs before her own.

As an adult, Joe listened to his mother, but didn't share much of what was going on in his own life with her. He saw how he had also picked up her people-pleasing pattern.

Joe had also felt much love and care from his father, but his dad tended to be critical and have a "right or wrong" way of seeing the world. Joe picked up this perfectionistic pattern, and until we began working together, this was the way he thought he had to be to survive and thrive in the world.

Given these past experiences, Joe saw how he could easily take on the beliefs that: I (and others) have to be perfect and "do it right," "I need to please others and put their needs before my own," and "I have to do a lot to prove I am good enough." He came to see that these beliefs, and the patterns/behaviors they generated, caused him to disconnect from himself.

As Joe worked on making time to connect with himself daily, and practiced accepting himself instead of judging and blaming himself, we also focused on shifting his beliefs to "I don't have to be perfect," "there is no right or wrong," and "my needs and desires are important."

We used the guided therapeutic meditation practices, daily affirmations (spoken, visual and written), and action steps Joe could take that were in alignment with these truths.

Implications and Results

After a few months of working together, Joe's neurological symptoms began to improve. He was taking more time to connect with himself daily through the guided practices and journaling. He began pushing himself less at work and he began setting boundaries and taking on fewer projects. He noticed he was catching his negative self-talk sooner, and switching it to more accepting language.

Today, Joe feels like he has much better work-life balance and he more easily sets boundaries at work. He's able to more confidently express his needs and desires with his wife, and share more of himself with his mom. He continues to make connecting with himself a priority, and he uses his tools to do so daily.

His self-talk has improved by leaps and bounds, he is much more accepting of himself and others, and he feels more peaceful.

He continues to make time for activities and supportive friendships that bring him joy.

His neurological symptoms continue to improve and, if they flare up, he reflects on where in his life he has fallen out of alignment again, and he makes changes accordingly.

In Joe's Own Words:

Since I began working with Tanya, I feel I have grown in so many ways that I would have never considered.

The thought that my illness could have stemmed from my deep commitment to self-criticism and lack of self-love, and martyring myself as a "beast of burden" had never occurred to me.

The onset of symptoms around Christmas of 2015 included visual and hearing loss, capped with facial paralysis.

After extensive work-ups from experts, a "professional opinion" of Multiple Sclerosis was all I had. Given there was no hard evidence pointing to this assumption, I proceeded to look elsewhere for answers.

On reflection, I absolutely believe my symptoms were the product of an unattainable goal of "perfection," extreme stress — and guilt for decisions and choices that didn't support that goal — and the fact that regardless of whether I succeeded or failed at a physical or mental endeavor, it was never good enough. This resulted in me physically breaking myself down, both in body and spirit.

I believe I achieved critical mass when I became ill with a recurring virus two months prior to the onset of my symptoms. Without a doubt I feel this perfect storm of personal behaviors, coupled with a trigger, led to my symptoms.

While working with Tanya over the past 10 months, my physical symptoms have continued to improve, and I feel I have made gains in all areas of my life.

Not only do I feel more at peace with my current circumstances and my contributions to such circumstances, but I have become a more patient and loving father, a more cooperative husband, and a compassionate caregiver.

I have also learned to give myself some slack, I expect progress and not perfection, and I love my life for what I have, and don't dwell on what I do not have.

Tanya's tools, especially the therapeutic meditation practices, are effective at helping me find positive daily mindsets, and rebounding daily during stressful episodes. They also quickly guide me to restful sleep at night.

I'm grateful for the guidance and tools Tanya has given me. - Joe

Chapter 2: Self-Acceptance & Compassion

Accepting all parts of you is necessary to healing your body and mind. — Tanya Penny

Why Is Self-Acceptance Necessary for Connection?

Before we dive into the self-connection areas, I believe it is important to have a little chat about self-acceptance and compassion.

Through my own experience, and in working with hundreds of clients, I've learned that the more we accept ourselves, the more we will want to *make* time to connect, and actually look forward to and enjoy our connection time. We often think we accept ourselves, but when we are willing to be honest and look deeper, we find that we only fully accept the parts of ourselves that we believe are "good," or even "perfect." We may try to connect, and then make the un-perfect parts wrong or bad; we then end up feeling even worse about ourselves and then we stop trying to connect altogether. I mean, come on. Who wants to connect when you beat yourself up and just make yourself feel even worse? Yeah, that's what I thought.

The truth is that we have been conditioned by our family, culture, media and peers to pick apart, criticize and reject any part of us that isn't perfect or "acceptable" to them. Again, refer back to reason #1 in The Truth About Self-Connection chapter on why we disconnect in the first place.

29

Let me paint you a picture with some personal examples…

- I am in third grade and being teased for wearing a bra. Yes, I hit puberty EARLY. I am also the first girl I know to get my period, and I hide it from everyone but my mother for more than a year. I am ashamed and begin hating my **body** and wanting to change (disconnect from) it.

- My mother is trying to talk to my dad about how she feels and what she desires, and she is crying (again). My dad gets very angry, yells, and starts smashing shit. I learn it is not safe to express my **desires or the emotion** of sadness. It feels safer, and we feel stronger, if we "stuff it" with behavioral choices that we hope will neutralize the painful emotions. I start stuffing my sadness with food, then alcohol and drugs, and the art of staying busy.

- No matter which or how many chores I do at home, or how good my grades are at school, my dad criticizes me, and I begin holding the **belief** that I never do enough and I'm never good enough.

- Growing up, I see and hear from magazines and TV commercials what I need to do and be in order for my **body** to be acceptable, and attractive to others. Be thin, but not too thin. Be sexy, but not slutty. Eat, but not too much and not certain foods, ever.

Be funny and smart, but not too funny or smart because it will make others feel less than or think you are too much. Pretend you like what others like and stuff what you really **desire** down into that empty hole of sadness that is inside you, so you can fit in and be liked. You get the picture.

- I am 15 years old and start dating an older guy. I get invited to my first drinking party. I drink to fit in, pass out, and then I am date-raped by the guy. He says that if I tell anyone or break up with him, he will deny it. He'll say I'm a slut and then no one else will want me. I believe him. I blame myself, continue to date and sleep with him for years, and only tell one friend. I hate, and despise, all of me. I gain 20 pounds and continue to drink (a lot) to stuff the **emotion** of pain I am feeling back down inside me. I don't know what else to do with it. I didn't learn healthy ways to feel and release my emotions. I just learned that negative ones are bad to have and express.

You can see from these examples why I might not accept myself — my emotions, feelings, desires, beliefs or my body — or even accept that there could be something bigger than me that "has my back."

Having Compassion for Yourself

As we do all of this inner work and discover more about ourselves, it's important to have compassion for ourselves. It may feel great to reconnect with yourself, and it may also feel hard or shitty somedays.

When we realize how, where or why we have disconnected from our true selves, it can cause us to feel sadness, anger, or grief. When this happens, remember to have compassion for yourself, and for what you are experiencing: all that you have experienced has brought you to this place on your healing journey.

Be grateful for your courage to make the changes in your life that help you to be healthy, and happy, and have the life you desire and deserve.

Tips, Tools and Inspired Actions:

Remember that awareness is the key to changing anything in your life. Let go of any judgement and reflect with compassion and curiosity on the following:

1. Rate, on a scale of 1-10, how much you feel you accept all parts of you at this moment. 0 = not at all. 10 = completely.

2. Reflect and write on the following questions:

   - What past experiences have contributed to your lack of self-acceptance? Make a list.

   - Have you noticed any judgement, shame or other emotions come up with the previous question? If yes, know that this is normal. Take a moment and write down what the voice in your head is saying, how you feel in your body, and any emotions arising. We will work with these emotions, judgements and beliefs later in the book.

3. Practice self-compassion — Look in the mirror daily, place your hand on your heart, and tell yourself how proud you are of you, all you have gone through, and accomplished up to this point in your life. Acknowledge it hasn't always been easy, but you had the courage to do it. You survived, and you are still walking the path, your unique healing path. Breathe in compassion and breathe out any shame, guilt, fear or judgement until it feels complete. Feel the compassion, gratitude and love you have for yourself. Open your eyes and go connect with, and be, your amazing self.

4. Guided Therapeutic Meditation Practice — Guided therapeutic meditation practices support you to have compassion for yourself and connect with and accept all parts of you. These practices are very nurturing and restful, and can be done in any position: lying down, seated, standing or moving. It's even okay to fall asleep and not hear a word, as they work on both a conscious and a subconscious level. For a sample guided therapeutic meditation practice, please visit: www.tanyapenny.com/cdy.

In the next chapter, I will outline the self-connection areas that represent opportunities for healing, and provide some tools for helping you move forward. We will then dive into each area, so you can begin the process of connecting with, and accepting, all parts of you so you can cultivate health, peace and happiness.

Self-acceptance and Compassion:

A Client Connection

Annik's Story

Annik was referred to me by a friend who had heard me speak at an online event. She was looking for support to heal anxiety, depression, body shame, insomnia, migraines, past trauma and Multiple Sclerosis. She wanted to heal the natural way and eventually wean herself off her migraine and pain medications.

Why She Came to See Me

Annik had experienced anxiety, depression, insomnia and migraines on and off for most of her life. She had had a traumatic childhood and a history of several abusive male relationships.

She used to be overweight as a child and teen, and even though she was at her ideal weight now, she continued to struggle with body dysmorphia.

Annick was diagnosed with Multiple Sclerosis in 2001 and had symptoms of numbness, weakness, and fatigue that kept her from working and completing other daily personal activities.

How We Worked Together

Annik and I began working together in the Vibrant Body & Abundant Life Mastery virtual group program where she began learning the Therapeutic Meditation Process and using the guided meditation practices and journaling exercises daily.

After a few months, we transitioned to also working together in private sessions via Skype each month.

The Issue at the Heart of the Matter

Over the course of our time together, I asked Annik to take time to connect with, and accept, all parts of herself daily.

I encouraged her to keep up a practice of reflecting and journaling and using guided therapeutic meditation practices in the morning or at midday, and again at bedtime as she fell asleep. She used these tools to listen to her body's messages, to understand, feel and release her emotions, to feel more rested and sleep better, to discover and shift the limiting beliefs that were causing her to push herself too hard mentally and physically, and to determine what in her past might have contributed to her having these beliefs and patterns.

Annik discovered a lot by using the self-connection process and tools daily. In reflecting on her past, she saw that she hadn't been shown much love or support by her parents while she was growing up.

Her mother was emotionally unavailable, cold, yelled a lot and threw things when she was angry. She often doled out "the silent treatment," and she favored Annik's sister.

Her mother kicked Annik out of the house when she was 18 and pregnant, and years later she turned her back again when Annik was physically abused by her boyfriend.

Annik's father was mostly absent and always working. He was emotionally unavailable, giving her financial support, but not showing love or saying, "I love you." He also had a bad temper and he drank a lot.

Not receiving the support she needed created a lot of insecurity, anxiety and fear. It also caused Annik to take on the beliefs that she wasn't worthy or lovable, she had to do everything by herself, she couldn't trust anyone, and that no one would support her (just abuse her).

It was no surprise that she attracted and stayed in relationships with men who were verbally and physically abusive, because she believed that was what she deserved.

How We Worked Together (Part 2)

Annik worked on using her Therapeutic Meditation Process tools to connect with, accept and give herself the support she hadn't received growing up.

She learned to listen to her body, acknowledge, accept, and feel her emotions, build her trust in "Something Bigger," shift her limiting beliefs, and plant the seeds of truth, including: "I am lovable and worthy, I am always loved and supported, I can trust others and receive support, and I don't have to do it all alone."

Annik also started taking inspired actions that were in alignment with her divine self.

Implications and Results

After several months of working together, Annik's emotional and physical symptoms began to slowly decrease.

She started to sleep better, and she felt less fatigued and anxious. She was beginning to accept and love herself more.

She was listening to her body and not pushing herself physically when her body said, "no."

Today, Annik manages her physical and emotional symptoms using her Therapeutic Meditation Process tools.

She hasn't had any MS symptoms for more than two years and she no longer takes pain or migraine medications.

Her self-acceptance and love has doubled for her body and all parts of herself.

If her patterns of people-pleasing, perfection or trying to be Superwoman and do it all alone show up, she is able to catch them faster and she uses her tools to shift into a healthy place of balance again.

She continues to practice setting and keeping healthy boundaries with others, and honoring her divine self.

Plus, she is moving into discovering and fully living her purpose to support others to heal too.

In Annik's Own Words

Working with Tanya has been incredibly life changing! I have made so much progress in the last 16 months! I honestly feel that I couldn't have done it without her support, guidance and accountability.

When we started working together, I'd just had a full hip replacement surgery at the age of 39 and this caused the Multiple Sclerosis to flare up.

My doctor wanted me to start taking disease-modifying drugs. I had also been taking a pain reliever and a medication for chronic migraines for 15 years.

I knew I wanted to heal and not use medications any longer. With Tanya by my side, I started to delve deeper into my emotional healing and I acquired many tools to support me.

After 15 years on my healing journey, I just had my first "normal" neurological exam!!! I am off all medications with no symptoms except fatigue (when I overdo it).

I am still working with Tanya to shift this "Superwoman" pattern. I am further living proof that the mind-body healing and the "natural way" not only work, but they are achievable by anyone looking to take their health into their own hands. I couldn't have done it without Tanya Penny.

Thank you, Tanya, from the bottom of my heart! I will be eternally grateful to your commitment to helping people heal the natural way.

– Annik

Chapter 3: The Self-Connection Process

Connecting with oneself can be the hardest and healthiest thing we can do in our lives. — Tanya Penny

My Healing Journey and Creating the Process

Through my own journey of healing anxiety, depression, insomnia, eating disorders, weight, various forms of abuse and Multiple Sclerosis, I have found that there are six areas of self-connection and four main tools to support us to re-connect with ourselves. I call this combination the Therapeutic Meditation Process® (TMP).

When you hear the word therapeutic, you may think of a person lying on a couch telling their problems to a counselor or a psychologist.

Or perhaps you think about someone being taken through a bunch of physical exercises by a physical or occupational therapist, so they can heal after surgery or an accident. In either case, it requires someone else to "do" the healing "to you," as opposed to you doing it to and for yourself.

I actually was, and still am, an occupational therapist, and I've also been on the receiving end of many counseling sessions in my lifetime. But, in this case, I am using the word *therapeutic* to imply a self-healing process.

And then there is the word meditation. You may have an image of a person seated with crossed legs and closed eyes trying to stop their thoughts or clear their mind. Good luck.

I believe the word meditation means being connected to all parts of you, including your "Something Bigger" (SB) — God, Source, Universe, or whatever you call it — all day long, in any position: walking, sitting, standing, lying down, etc., and always acting from this place of connection and guidance.

Before we dive into the process, I would like to share a little about my experience and how I arrived at it.

As I mentioned in the introduction, I stopped using western medicine in 2007 and began my deeper search for what would ultimately heal me. I prayed daily for guidance and the answer I was seeking. I started using acupuncture, diet, massage, supplements, and chiropractic care. I believe they all had their place and were each a part of my healing puzzle.

In 2008, I was asked to be part of an eight-week study with Boise State University for people who had a diagnosis of multiple sclerosis, and who were willing to use a meditation practice called Integrative Restoration® (iRest). Participants were asked to attend a group class each week where we were taught the steps of the practice, and then were taken through a guided meditation practice while lying down. I left the first class knowing that this practice was profound, and an important missing piece of my puzzle.

I had suffered from anxiety since I was a young child, even though I wasn't formally diagnosed with generalized anxiety disorder until I was in my early twenties.

I remember being five years old and lying on my grandmother's couch trying to take a nap. I was sobbing silently because I was so worried and afraid about my parents, who were constantly fighting. This anxiety, and a feeling of being unsafe in the world, grew as I got older, likely because I was teased at school, and criticized at home.

My mom and dad separated numerous times, and I was sexually abused by several boys. As I mentioned earlier, I started self-medicating, first with food, then alcohol and drugs, sex and men, and even over-exercising. I'd do anything to keep from feeling the anxiety, fear, and self-loathing I felt inside.

When I walked out of the first iRest® class, I felt at peace in both body and mind for the first time in my life. I also felt connected to spirit, though I didn't know that at the time. This feeling lasted for a few hours. After class, I went to my book club and friends jokingly asked, "what did you do with Tanya?!"

I went to bed feeling Zen, but still awoke the next morning with my heart racing with panic, as I did every day. I wanted the feeling of peace I had had the day before, so I decided to play the guided iRest practice CD the group organizers had given participants for the study. After 30 minutes, I was back to my peaceful Zen place again.

From that point forward, I used this guided meditation practice every day, sometimes two or three times a day, depending on how I felt, physically and mentally. The peace and overall well-being I felt was something the western medication or self-medicating behaviors never gave me. Plus, I had no awful side effects to deal with!

After eight weeks of using this practice daily I not only noticed that I felt more peaceful, but there were many other positive benefits as well. I had been suffering from insomnia and nightmares since I was a child. It used to take me one-to-two hours to fall asleep, even with sleeping pills, and I would wake three-to-five times on average during the night, after which I would lie awake at least an hour. Then my alarm would go off. I began using the iRest practice at bedtime, falling asleep before the practice was through, and sleeping though the night — except for getting up once to use the bathroom… but I'd fall back to sleep almost right away.

Now let's get into the really amazing details. Due to the MS, I had lost vision in my right eye, and I had debilitating fatigue, weakness and numbness in my right arm and leg, as well as neck pain. All of these would normally lessen by several degrees on a scale of 1-10 after I underwent a guided practice. It inspired me to get trained in iRest. I knew that if this practice was key for me and *my* healing process, then it would be for others, too.

After my training, I began a program at the rehabilitation hospital and started using the guided meditation practice with my occupational therapy clients, and teaching it. I trained two other therapists to do the same.

During this time, I also started studying mind-body healing philosophy through Louise Hay's books and Hay House Radio speakers, Dr. Carolyn Myss and Dr. Mona Lisa Schulz. They expounded upon the idea that my negative or self-limiting thoughts about myself and the world, and the negative emotions that they caused (and I stuffed), were the underlying causes of all of the negative symptoms I had been experiencing.

I started journaling, using positive affirmations and other practices that supported me to connect, feel, and release daily.

I also created and recorded specific guided meditation practices to feel and release my negative emotions, shift my self-limiting beliefs, and plant the seeds for what I desired in my life in terms of health, relationships, money, purpose, passions, and, most importantly, self-acceptance and love.

I began listening to these meditations several times a day.

I was also guided to get trained in yoga therapy. Before I was diagnosed with MS I was doing "gym yoga" for exercise.

While I was experiencing the numbness and weakness from the MS, I couldn't do the intense yoga, so I started going to a gentle yoga class.

I eventually became a yoga teacher. It really helped me to create a positive connection with my body. I learned to move in a gentle way, and honor my body, rather than push it to extremes like I had done in the past.

The more I used these tools daily to connect with and accept all of me, the better I felt mentally, physically, and emotionally.

By 2010, I no longer experienced the MS symptoms, and I didn't struggle with weight and body shame, or debilitating depression and anxiety. It was a miracle, and I knew I had to share it all with others.

I felt I had finally found my purpose and reclaimed the health and passion for life that I had lost so many years earlier.

I also knew I had to leave my safe, secure western medicine hospital job and open my own practice so I could fully share all my tools, teach my mind-body-spirit healing philosophy, and discuss all 10 Vibrant Body & Abundant Life Keys, which I will share in my next book. ☺

Therapeutic Meditation Process ® (TMP)

The Therapeutic Meditation Process ® (TMP) includes six areas of self-connection and four main tools to support you to connect with, and accept, all of the six self-connection areas on a daily basis.

The Self-Connection Areas:

1. **Desires.** What you focus on grows. Every day you can choose to focus on what you desire to do, have, and be, rather than on what is not working in your life. What do you desire in all seven areas of your life—self, health, love and relationships, spirituality, passions, money and material goods, and purpose? Focus on them daily with ease while believing you deserve it ALL, and in divine time you will receive it, or the "OR BETTER" version.

2. **Breath.** Your breath is a barometer, always letting you know how you are feeling mentally and emotionally. It is also a powerful tool to relax the body and mind.

3. **Body and Feelings.** Connecting with and accepting your body and its feelings is important, as it is also a barometer that lets you know when you are in or out of balance in your life. When the body has negative feelings or symptoms it is letting you know that you are out of alignment or balance in one or more areas of your life. Learn the basics of mind-body healing philosophy, and how to understand the messages your body is giving you, so you can heal and be healthy and happy.

4. **Emotions** Perhaps like most people, you have been taught to ignore or stuff your emotions. On the flip side, perhaps you get stuck in your emotions, letting them consume you and keep you from taking action. Learn to acknowledge, accept, feel, and release your emotions in healthy ways to heal and maintain your health.

5. **Thoughts and Beliefs.** What we think and believe about ourselves, our health, love, money, work, etc., creates our reality. Most of the time we are not even aware of our thoughts in these areas. Discover your self-limiting

thoughts and beliefs and learn tools to accept and shift them to receive what you desire in all areas of your life.

6. **"Something Bigger" (SB).** Not being fully connected to our "Something Bigger" (Universe, God, Nature, etc.), and believing we are all alone — or are only able to receive guidance and support for some things and not *all* things — causes a lot of stress, anxiety and, eventually, illness.

I will be diving into each of these areas in more detail in the following chapters of this book. Get ready!

The Self-Connection Tools

Here are the tools I believe you need to use in order to connect with and heal your self:

1. **Mind-Body Healing Philosophy** — Mind-body healing philosophy looks at the underlying emotional and mental causes of physical symptoms in the body — including pain, excessive or insufficient weight, and illness.

2. **Reflection / Journaling / Writing** - Journaling questions and writing exercises help you to build self-awareness and acceptance, understand and release negative emotions, and uncover patterns or beliefs that are holding you back from making positive life changes and healing.

3. **Guided Meditation Practices** — Guided meditation practices include all the above areas of self-connection. These practices are very nurturing and restful, and can be done in any position: lying down, seated, standing or moving. It is even okay if you fall asleep, drift in and out, and don't hear a word, as they work on both a conscious and a subconscious level. You can find a sample guided TMP practice to start using at: www.tanyapenny.com/cdy.

4. **Other Tools and Daily Practices** — Through my own experiences and healing journey, I have created other daily practices and tips that I will be sharing with you in this book, so you can fully connect, accept, and heal.

As we move through the following chapters on all of the self-connection areas, I will be incorporating these tools for you to use so you can connect with the Divine You each and every day to cultivate more health, peace, and happiness… just like me!

Okay! Let's dive in!!!

The Self-Connection Process:

A Client Connection

Belinda's Story

Belinda had previously had a bout with thyroid cancer and she knew she needed to make some changes in her life so that she didn't get it — or any other chronic illness — again.

Why She Came to See Me

Belinda found me through a free live virtual class I was hosting. She wanted to heal her anxiety, brain fog, fatigue, and increase her self-confidence, so she could be more successful in her business. As a wife and the mother of two adult children, she knew she had a hard time setting and keeping boundaries with her family, as well as with other people in her extended family. The over-giving of her time and energy kept her from having the time to focus on her desires.

How We Worked Together

Belinda and I decided that the best way for us to work together was in private sessions on the phone, as well as in the virtual group program I was running for business owners. We met one or two times a month for 12 sessions, and she also participated in the live group classes in the business program.

The Issue at the Heart of the Matter

Through our sessions and in using the tools of the process to reflect, Belinda began to see all the ways she had become disconnected from her true self, and how the symptoms she had were at the root of this. Belinda was the youngest child in has family and, as she had grown up, she hadn't felt like she belonged. She had stepped into the role of the fixer or mediator to get attention, love and acceptance. Now, as an adult, when people had problems, or issues arose between family members, she felt responsible for helping them to sort it all out. If she didn't, she felt guilty, and worried that they wouldn't like her. And if she tried to help them, but couldn't, she also felt like she was not good enough and that the problem was all her fault.

Belinda's parents had had a rocky marriage and she had witnessed her dad being abusive to her mother. They divorced when Belinda was seven years old. She didn't see her dad very much and, when she did, he would drink and not be emotionally present with her. This also added to her feelings of unworthiness. It wasn't surprising that she married a man who also drank, and was emotionally unavailable, and that she stuffed how she felt and what she wanted in order to please him, so she wouldn't get abused or be abandoned. At least he was physically present for her, unlike her father had been. As we continued to work together, Belinda realized how much anger had arisen as a result of her stuffing who she was and what she desired.

Belinda had a harsh inner critic who beat her up for not being good enough, and also made her feel anxious with all the pressure it was putting on her to do everything perfectly. This negative self-talk was caused by not feeling accepted, lovable or worthy growing up. This perfection part of her was also holding her back in her business. If she didn't feel good enough, or worthy, then how could she help others?

She realized these unhealthy patterns of perfection, doing to please others, plus trying to be Superwoman and fix other's problems needed to change so she could make time for herself, heal, and have the confidence to support others to heal too. Over the course of our time together, Belinda began taking time to connect with and accept all parts of herself daily through reflecting, journaling, and using guided therapeutic meditation practices. She also used these tools to continue to reflect on her past and how it had contributed to her current health issues.

Belinda used the process to help her to understand the messages her body was giving her, acknowledge, feel and release emotions of anxiety, insecurity, anger and grief, and shift the beliefs that were keeping her stuck in her unhealthy patterns: "I can't express what I desire, I have to do it perfectly, I'm responsible for fixing others' problems." The goal was to plant new beliefs and desires: "It's safe to speak my truth, I'm not responsible for others' problems or lives, I'm lovable and worthy no matter what I do." And, also, to connect with Something Bigger to feel safe and supported.

Belinda started expressing what she wanted and how she felt with her husband. She began setting boundaries with family members, so she had more time and energy to heal and get clear on what she desired in her life.

Implications and Results

After working together for a year, Belinda's brain fog completely dissolved. Her negative self-talk decreased, and she was feeling less anxious, more worthy and confident. Her energy returned, and her thyroid numbers were good, with no sign of cancer returning.

She is expressing more of who she is with everyone in her life and feels she has a healthy balance of supporting others while focusing on her desires. She doesn't get sucked up in family drama anymore and lets them all fix their own problems. She also just completed the Therapeutic Meditation Process Teacher Certification and plans to weave it into her business, so she can teach it to others.

In Belinda's Own Words

I'm so grateful that I found Tanya and decided to invest in working with her.

Learning the Therapeutic Meditation Process and coaching with Tanya has proved invaluable. I feel healthy, clear and energized. I feel I am making the changes I need to make so that cancer will not return. I am finally living my life for me and expressing who I am with confidence.

I love and trust myself more than I ever could've imagined. I'm now excited to teach this life-changing process to others. Thank you, Tanya Penny!

– Belinda

Chapter 4: Your Desires

What you focus on grows. Plant the seeds for what you desire and water them daily. – Tanya Penny

Truth: What We Take Time to Focus on in Our Life Grows

One of the biggest ways we disconnect from ourselves and our spirit occurs when we don't take the time to set intentions daily and focus on our desires. This is also the cause of unhappiness, depression, and anger, and it can often lead to illness.

Have you recently (or ever) taken the time to reflect on what you desire in ALL areas of your life?

Perhaps, like many, you say you don't have the time to reflect, much less *act* on having what you desire.

I believe many of us use time as a sexy excuse that is really hiding our... FEARS. Here are some of the most common fears that keep us from discovering and/or acting on our desires:

- What if I discover what I desire and then have to make uncomfortable, hard or scary changes?

- What if I realize my relationship, job, etc. is not what I really want, and I need to leave it?

- What if I discover, express and act on my desires and it upsets or draws criticism from my parents, partner, kids, friend, neighbor, dog, etc.?

- What if I don't believe I have the smarts, skills, money or time to follow through and it just makes me feel more depressed and disappointed in myself and my life?

No wonder we don't want to take the time to focus on our desires. Taking those steps forward requires a LOT of courage, a deep sense of self-acceptance and worth, PLUS the support and accountability of others.

In looking back, I realize that I had a tendency to stuff my desires deep down inside me in the context of intimate relationships.

My deep fear of causing conflict and being abandoned would often keep me from doing or saying anything that might make the other person angry enough to ultimately leave me. I have worked on healing and shifting these fears a LOT, but to this day, I will sometimes find myself holding back from expressing my desires with my sweetie.

Remember, it can take time to shift your fears, and it requires you to have patience and compassion for yourself during the process.

When I start working with a client, I ask them to reflect on and describe their desires in all seven life areas:

1. **Your Self:**   In your relationship with yourself, how do you feel about, talk to/about, and treat you?

2. **Your Health**:   What shape are you in mentally, physically, and emotionally?

3. **Your Spirituality**: What is your connection to, and relationship with, your "Something Bigger" (God, Universe, Source, etc.)?

4. **Your Relationship(s)**: What are your relationships like with your partner, kids, parents, siblings, friends, co-workers, and healers?

5. **Your Passions**:   What are your hobbies? What do you do for fun? What lights you up?

6. **Your Purpose**: Your work and career. What would you jump out of bed for, and what would you love to get paid to do every day?

7. **Your Money and Material Goods**: Where would you like to live, what would you like to have, etc.? How much money would you like to make in order to have all you desire?

I tell my clients to dream big, to act as if there are no limits on their time, money, and skills AND to pretend no one will care. As they do this exercise, I also tell them to be aware of, and write down, any negative or self-limiting beliefs and voices that chime in and say things like:

- Who do you think you are?

- Where the hell will you get the money?

- How on Earth will you find the time?

- What will _____ (fill in the blank) think of you?

- You're not smart enough or talented enough

- People will think you are weird or a fraud

- You will be criticized, rejected or embarrassed

- It will be hard, you don't know how

- AND lots of other bullshit like _____ (fill in the blank)

Ahhh! Why so many negative voices? Why is this so hard? You likely already have your own answer to that question but here are three suggestions:

1. You didn't see or hear your parents follow their desires.

2. You heard one or more of those statements while growing up and it has stopped you dead in your tracks.

3. You are carrying a ton of self-limiting and negative beliefs that make you think it is not possible, so why bother going there?

While I was growing up:

- I saw my mom try to express her desires and my dad often blew up because of it. So of course, I took on the belief that, "Expressing your desires is not safe, and it causes conflict." I acted that out in my intimate relationships for a long time.

- I saw both of my parents work at jobs they didn't really like, but they didn't feel they could do anything else.

- I heard statements like, "You can't have everything you want, money doesn't grow on trees, you have to be really smart to do that" etc.

The key is to move forward and do it anyway. Regardless of the negative things your inner voice says, keep going. Carve out time in your schedule to reflect on each of the key areas in life, even if it's only for 5-10 minutes a day. Write down what you desire in each area.

Allow yourself to dream big. Take baby steps towards those desires daily. Get support from those who believe in you, and don't bother telling those who don't. Learn and use tools to shift those negative voices, fears and self-limiting beliefs (see chapter 8), as they are the only things truly holding you back from your desires. Really.

Tips, Tools and Inspired Actions:

Remember that what you focus on grows! I recommend that you carve time out in your schedule to complete all of the tasks listed below within the next week, two tops. Then show up with compassion for and curiosity around what you find or experience. You and your desires are worth it!

1. Rate, on a scale of 1-10, how connected you feel to your desires at this time. (0 = not at all. 10 = completely, deeply connected). You may want to rate each of the seven life areas, as you might feel very connected and active in some, and not at all in another.

2. Reflect and write: In what life area(s) have you been ignoring or stuffing your desires down below the radar of your daily life? Why? Block at least one hour in your schedule to reflect on your desires in all of the seven life areas mentioned above. If two 30-minute blocks work better, then go for it. What is important is that you make the time available and do it! During this time, show up, and set aside your concerns and fears related to money, time or what others will think. Dream big... as if anything is possible. I recommend that you set aside one

notebook page for each life area. Or you can create a document on your computer, instead. As you do this, be aware of any judgements, fears, limiting beliefs or negative voices that come in when writing your desires. Remember, this is normal. Instead of ignoring them, take a moment and write them down. I recommend you keep a separate piece of paper or document for "Self-Limiting Beliefs." We will come back and deal with these little gremlins later.

3. Next, write a positive statement in the present tense (as if it's already true) for each life area. Use an emotional or feeling word to start the sentence. I recommend that you then write each desire sentence on its own index card (I use pastel colored index cards).

Examples:

Self: I always love myself and follow my desires

Health: I love being peaceful, happy, and healthy

Spirituality: I'm always trusting and following my Something Bigger (insert your word)

Relationships: I love having honest, supportive, and fun relationships

Purpose: I enjoy doing what I love and getting paid abundantly

Passions: I am always taking time and money to do my passions

Money: I have an abundance of money to do / be / have all I desire

4. For each desire, write down a list of one-to-three small, inspired action steps you can take in the next week or month to move towards that desire. I recommend that you write these on the same index card that matches each desire sentence (and on the same side) and also schedule the action steps in your calendar to make sure you actually do them. ☺

    Some of us need even more support to actually do them (Me included!). You can ask a friend to be your accountability buddy, or you may even want the support of a coach. To find out about all of the ways I can support you, please visit www.tanyapenny.com.

5. Now, back to those little gremlins. Take your list of "Self-Limiting Beliefs" and write an opposite more positive belief for each one. Note: You do not need to believe the opposite you write at this time.

    Example: "I don't have enough money or time" vs. "I have all the money and time that I need."

Here is a list of inspired actions I created for you to take daily. Yes, I mean moving forward every day of your life. I promise that, if you do, these actions will support you to focus on and receive your desires in divine time. So, without further ado, I invite you to:

- Take the desire sentences you listed above, an opposing self-limiting belief, and its opposite, and use them in a guided therapeutic meditation practice one-to-three times daily. Feel free to insert a different one each day, or rotate them. Do whatever feels "right" to you.

- You can also set an intention or two related to your desires and inspired action steps when doing the guided practice. Perhaps you would like to set an intention to connect with courage, trust, or clarity. Perhaps to release the emotion of fear or some other "negative" emotion that is holding you back from taking actions towards your desires. Maybe you are tired and want to feel more rested, so you can take your inspired actions. If you are dealing with a negative feeling in the body (pain, depression, weakness, headache, etc.) that is holding you back today, you can set an intention to understand it and release it, so you feel well enough to take an inspired action.

  Download a sample guided therapeutic meditation practice at www.tanyapenny.com/cdy.

- Create a "Desires" board, book or wall. Cut out and post pictures and words on it that relate to each of your desires. Make sure you keep it somewhere visible where you will see it several times each day. Mine is on my home office wall. I also recommend that you take at least one picture and/or word and paste it on the back of the index card with a matching desire. You can find a sample of mine at www.tanyapenny.com/cdy.

- Take five minutes or so to look at and read each desire on your index cards every morning. Read, then close your eyes and visualize yourself living it, as if it were already true, right in this moment. Do this again before you go to sleep each night.

- Look at the inspired actions steps you listed on your desire cards. Is there an action you can take today to bring you closer to your desires? Breathe in courage, put one foot (or finger) in front of the other, and DO IT NOW!

- Every morning, set one-to-three intentions for the day that are related to one or more of your desires. Say them aloud and/or write them down. This will help you create a specific focus for the day that keeps reminding you about what you truly desire, and it will help you take actions that lead in that direction. Example: If your desire statement is "I am healthy, happy, and peaceful" you might have an intention to move your body for 30 minutes, meditate for 15-30 minutes and spend 30 minutes doing something you find fun and enjoyable.

Self-Connection and Your Desires:

A Client Connection

Daniel's Story

I met Daniel through a meditation class designed to help university music students decrease performance anxiety. Daniel wanted support to heal his anxiety, eating disorder, and negative self-talk.

Why He Came to See Me

Daniel knew his anxiety and negative self-talk were holding him back in school, and keeping him from performing at his highest capacity. He sought my assistance to help him move forward beyond the self-imposed boundaries that had been holding him back.

How We Worked Together

Daniel and I worked together in the University group classes to heal his performance anxiety, and then he wanted to work together privately to receive more support to heal his eating disorder and past trauma.

The Issue at the Heart of the Matter:

Daniel had had a difficult childhood. He had been verbally and physically bullied a lot in school. He also didn't feel very accepted by his family, and he was verbally abused there, as well. This caused him to feel a lot of shame and anxiety. Being treated this way also created in him unhealthy patterns of people-pleasing and trying to be perfect. Maybe if he could be perfect and please others, he would get the approval, acceptance and love he desired from his peers and family?

Now, as an adult, Daniel had extreme anxiety at school and while performing. He was afraid of making mistakes and being criticized or embarrassed. He also continued to fall into patterns of people-pleasing, and he had a hard time setting boundaries with classmates, friends and family. He was constantly pushing himself mentally and physically to be "good enough." All of this work and pressure left very little time for Daniel to connect with himself in a positive way. He saw how the eating disorder was a way for him to feel in control, but it also caused him a tremendous amount of shame.

Over the course of our time together, I asked Daniel to carve out time to connect with himself daily through reflecting and writing five-to-10 minutes a day, and using a guided therapeutic meditation practice in the morning, before tests and performances, and again at bedtime as he fell asleep. Using these tools helped him to begin accepting himself, to feel and release emotions of shame and anxiety, and shift the limiting beliefs that had been causing him to get stuck in the patterns of perfection and people-pleasing. His internal mantra had been: "I'm not good enough, there is something wrong with me, if I make a mistake I'll be hurt. I have to be perfect and please others to stay safe." We worked to replace that by planting the seeds for his desires, and helping a new truth to flourish: "I don't have to be perfect, it's okay to make mistakes, I love and accept myself for who I am, I'm worthy and lovable, I'm safe and capable of sticking up for myself, it's necessary to set boundaries with others, I'm important and always making time to care for me."

Implications and Results:

After a few months of working together, Daniel's performance anxiety started to decrease. He was feeling more confident performing, and doing better in his classes. He was setting boundaries with friends and family. He noticed he was catching his negative self-talk sooner and switching it to be more accepting. He was taking more time to connect with himself daily through the guided practices and journaling.

Today, Daniel takes time to connect daily, he is much more accepting of himself, and he honors his strengths and abilities. He is better about blocking his time to have balance, despite a very busy schedule. He speaks truthfully and authentically, and he sets good boundaries with friends and family.

He cares less about what people say or think of him, and he has stopped talking to anyone who is negative. His eating disorder is in remission and he feels he has solid tools to deal with any anxiety and shame if it arises. His confidence and feelings of worthiness have grown by leaps and bounds, and Daniel is now working on his second Master's Degree, this one in Music Therapy.

In Daniel's Own Words:

"My experience with Tanya has been one of true success.

Tanya has taught me to use the Therapeutic Meditation Process as a way to expose and cope with my performance anxiety. She has also given me the tools to heal verbal and physical abuse, and, most importantly, to heal a relapse of my eating disorder that threatened my career.

Using her tools, I have released so much shame and increased my confidence. My eating disorder is back in full remission, and I'm back to my normal, healthy weight.

I had to have back surgery, and using Therapeutic Meditation Process saved me from having to go through rehab. I was mobile and walking again within two weeks, up to two miles a day.

Tanya Penny's work is one of true importance and I recommend working with her with the highest regard."

– Daniel

Chapter 5: Your Breath

Your breath is your barometer, letting you know if you are in or out of balance with your true Self. — Tanya Penny

As you know, your breath is what keeps you alive. It is also a barometer for you, letting you know if you are in or out of balance — mentally, physically and emotionally.

Even more, your breath can be used as a powerful tool to relax the mind and body, feel grounded, connect with your self, and feel and release your emotions.

The Breath, Your Barometer

Are you aware that you hold your breath? We all do to some extent. Some of us do it a lot. You may hold your breath when you feel a "negative" emotion — overwhelm, anxiety, fear, or anger. You may hold it when you are over-exerting yourself physically or mentally. Maybe you hold your breath when you cry, or are trying not to.

I had a sleep study done years ago and found out that I was holding my breath and waking 30 times during the night. No wonder I felt fatigued, even when I was "sleeping" for between seven and eight hours every night!

When you hold your breath the cells in your body contract and don't get the oxygen they need.

Over time, chronic breath-holding creates more and more tension in the body and can cause headaches, increased blood pressure, digestion issues and even pain.

What is the quality of your breath? When I started down the path of alternative healing, I began to meditate, and that's when I became aware of how short and choppy my breath often was. I learned later that this is a sign of anxiety, usually present in those with past trauma — which is pretty much everyone.

As always, awareness is key. You can start tuning in to what your breath is telling you at this very moment. See what it is telling you about your current physical, mental and emotional state. Then keep reading to learn tools for using your breath to: relax your mind and body, feel grounded, *feel*, release your emotions and support your body to heal.

Tips, Tools and Inspired Actions:

Remember that awareness is the key to changing anything in your life. Let go of any judgement or perfection when reflecting on what follows.

1. On a scale of 0-10, rate, how aware of, and how connected you are, to your breath (0 = never, 10 = all the time).

2. Reflect and write about the following:

   - Check in with your breath right now. Close your eyes, and notice if it is short, deep, choppy, or smooth.

   - Do you notice that you hold your breath?

   - Are there certain situations that cause you to hold your breath?

   - Do you hold your breath when you are with certain people?

   - Do you have any past trauma that may cause you to hold your breath? Perhaps the experience of being bullied, criticized, or teased? Have you experienced physical or sexual abuse?

3. Breath Connection Exercise (Four Options):

   - Follow your breath as it comes into your nostrils, into your throat, into your chest, and down into your belly, and then follow it back out through your mouth or nose.

- Do not attempt to change or manipulate your breath in any way (Note that the simple act of attending to the breath automatically changes it).

- Stay here as long as it feels right to you. You may decide not to experience any further options (Especially if you're doing this while driving, standing, or talking).

When you're ready you might also add these options:

- Bring attention to your belly and feel and follow your belly's rising and falling during each inhalation and exhalation. Stay here as long as it feels right to you. You may also want to place your hands on your belly.

- Silently count each rising (inhalation) and each falling (exhalation) of your belly. It's recommended to start at one and count up to 10 if you are doing this during the day. It's also best to start at 10 and count backwards at bed-time. If you forget the number or become distracted, then start over at one (or 10) again. Continue until you get your desired result.

- Breathe in a positive emotion, feeling, or thought and breathe out the "negative" or opposite one. Do this until you feel a shift.

4. Guided Therapeutic Meditation Practice: Listen to a guided TMP 1-3x/day to connect with your breath, feel and hear what it is telling you, and release stress and heal. Find a sample practice at: www.tanyapenny.com/cdy.

5. Use your breath to decrease and alleviate your symptoms. When you have one of the following symptoms, try the breath exercise given above.

- **"Negative" Feelings.** Use your breath to feel and release negative feelings or symptoms — pain, headache, fatigue, weakness, nausea, etc. Close your eyes and follow your breath into your nostrils, chest and belly, then back out through your mouth or nose. Think about breathing in peace, happiness or relaxation and breathing out the "negative" emotion you are feeling. Do at least 10 rounds of this, or continue until you feel a shift in your emotion.

- **"Negative" Emotions.** Use your breath to feel and release negative emotions, such as anxiety, overwhelming worry, anger, sadness, etc. Close your eyes and follow your breath into your nostrils, chest and belly, then back out through your mouth or nose. Think about breathing in peace, happiness or relaxation and breathing out the "negative" emotions you are feeling. Do at least 10 rounds of this, orcontinue until you fcel a shift in your cmotion.

- **Digestion Issues.** If you have problems with digestion (gas, bloating, heartburn, etc.), take a few moments before each meal and close your eyes, then follow your breath in and out for 10 rounds. Continue to eat slowly and consciously breathe while you eat.

- **Weight**. Excess weight is often due to stress, which affects your cortisol levels and your metabolism. Take a few moments before each meal, close your eyes, then breathe in and out 10 rounds to release stress. You may even want to think about breathing in peace, joy or relaxation and breathing out stress or any other negative emotion you know you tend to stuff, as weight gain can also be due to holding onto these negative emotions (anger, sadness, guilt, shame, etc.).

- **High Blood Pressure**. Set a reminder in your calendar for morning, midday, after work and at bedtime to close your eyes and complete 10 rounds of breathing. You may also add a reminder to do a round before and after a "stressful" event.

- **Insomnia**. When falling asleep at night (or if you awaken and have trouble getting back to sleep), count the number of times your belly rises and falls, starting at 10 and counting down to 1. If you lose count or notice your mind drifting to other thoughts, start again at 10. Continue until you fall asleep.

Over time, the practice of noticing your breath will become more natural and you will begin to pick up on the distinctions that can point the way to greater personal sensitivity and awareness.

Although you will notice differences in your emotional state right away, it may take time for the full impact of the process to become evident.

Be patient with yourself. And remember to breathe!

Self-Connection and Your Breath:

A Client Connection

Diane's Story

Diane had recently been told she had "possible" Multiple Sclerosis and she was seeking to manage and heal her symptoms of fatigue, tingling, numbness, insomnia and anxiety using alternative healing methods. She was a wife and mother, and she worked part-time as a healer.

Why She Came to See Me

Diane found me by coming to a free live community class I was hosting. She was worried that her symptoms would affect her ability to take care of her home and daughter and interfere with her ability to serve her clients.

She was aware that she had a harsh inner critic, and that she criticized her husband and daughter. She wanted to be more positive with herself and others. She made little time to take care of herself, as she was always giving to her family and clients, and she knew this needed to change.

Diane's stress would shoot through the roof when she was dealing with her family and some of her clients. She sought me out to help her feel more peaceful and balanced in all situations, with all people, and not take on other people's emotions or problems.

How We Worked Together

Diane and I decided that best way for us to begin working together was through private sessions in person. We saw each other twice a month, and then moved to once a month after three months. We focused on one or two self-connection areas of the Therapeutic Meditation Process each session, and then Diane would practice using her tools between sessions while also working on the other inspired actions I suggested.

The Issue at the Heart of the Matter:

Over the course of our time together, I asked Diane to take time to connect with all parts of herself daily through reflecting, journaling, and using a guided therapeutic meditation practice before seeing her clients or midday and at bedtime. Also, I recommended she use these tools to look at her past and how it might have contributed to the unhealthy patterns of people pleasing, perfection and trying to be Superwoman that were causing her to disconnect from her true self.

In reflecting, she saw her mother had a habit of self-criticism and criticizing others, and that she was a people pleaser and tended to over-give to others. She was also extremely anxious. Diane also saw that she tried to please her mother, so she would get praise and love (and less criticism).

Diane's dad worked a lot and didn't spend much time with her or the family while she was growing up. Even though she knew he loved her, he didn't really express his love or emotions. She didn't see her parents express or share their emotions with each other either.

Given her experiences and what was modeled for her growing up, Diane realized why she tended to over-work, over-give to others, not know how to deal with her own emotions, and be critical of herself and others. She held the beliefs that "I'm not good enough, I have to be perfect, I have to please others to get love, I can't express my emotions, and I have to work hard."

Diane used the Therapeutic Meditation Process to help her understand the messages that her numbness and tingling were bringing her, to acknowledge, feel and release her emotions in healthy ways, and to shift the beliefs that were keeping her stuck in unhealthy patterns that caused her to disconnect from her true self.

One of her favorite mini-practices to use when she felt anxious was breathing *in* peace or calmness, and breathing *out* anxiety or overwhelm. She also used the tools to plant new beliefs and desires: "I'm always good enough, it's okay to express my emotions, I have to make time for myself every day, I love and accept myself just as I am, I don't have to work hard to please or be worthy." She also started asking for more support with the housework from her husband and daughter, saying no to others when she needed time for herself, and learning the balance of supporting her clients, but not taking on their emotions or problems.

Implications and Results

After working with me for few months, Diane's numbness and tingling began to dissolve. She was sleeping better, and she felt more energized. She noticed she was speaking to herself and others with kindness instead of criticism. She takes a break between client sessions and picking her daughter up at school by using a guided therapeutic meditation practice that helps her feel more rested while releasing stress and/or negative emotions. She continues to ask for more support from others and saying no so she has time to care for herself. She continues to practice sharing how she truly feels and what she desires with her family and friends. Overall, Diane feels more relaxed, peaceful, healthy, balanced and happy with herself and her life.

In Diane's Own Words:

"I'm so happy I made myself a priority, went to Tanya's free community class, and then decided to coach with her to heal anxiety and the other physical symptoms I was experiencing.

Learning the Therapeutic Meditation Process has been a huge blessing in my life. It has not only helped me to heal physically, but also mentally and emotionally.

I have never been able to meditate, but Tanya's guided practices are so easy and soothing that I drift right off. I also love using mini-breath breaks throughout the day to feel more peaceful and to relax my body.

By showing up and making more time for my own self-care, I am actually able to be more present, positive and supportive of others in my life, personally, and as a healer. I feel like I am finally living the peaceful, healthy and balanced life I've always wanted. Thank you from the bottom of my heart Tanya!"

- *Diane*

Chapter 6: Your Body Feelings

Your body never lies. Instead of resisting it, learn to listen to its messages. — Tanya Penny

Learning to re-connect, accept and understand your body and its feelings is essential to healing your illness. Your body is always giving you clues, letting you know if you are in or out of alignment with your authentic, true, soul self. It will never lie to you. Start treating it like your ally or friend and it will support you to heal.

What Are Feelings?

Before we dive into the topic of connecting with your body and its feelings, I feel it's important to share what I mean when I use the word feelings. In my world and work, feelings mean what you feel in your body, the physical symptoms you are experiencing — pain, fatigue, weakness, headache, excess weight, cramping, etc.

Why is Connecting with Your Body Important?

Your body and its feelings are parts of you. You don't ever want to ignore or reject any part of you. Period. As with any self-connection area, acceptance is key, as whatever we

rsists, and — like a lot of children will do — it
s more obtrusive until it finally gets our attention.

Your body and its feelings represent one of your internal
messengers. They are not good or bad, right or wrong.
They simply give you information.

When the body feels "good" and healthy, and no symptoms
are present, it means you are in alignment with your divine
self.

But when you are having "negative" symptoms or illness,
that means your body is giving you clues as to where in
your life you are out of alignment, and which emotions and
beliefs you are holding that are causing you to be out of
alignment.

Why Am I Disconnected from My Body?

Are you disconnected from your body? Do you try to
ignore the negative symptoms when they pop up? Perhaps
you even hate your body, or see it as the enemy? If so, then
you are like me and most of the clients I work with.

From a young age, many of us were taught to ignore our
bodies and listen instead to the conditioned, egoic mind. If
we had a negative feeling or symptom, the norm was to
ignore it, and pretend it was not there…until it became
really "loud," and stopped us from functioning; then we
would go to the doctor.

A client shared with me a memory of being sick one day
when she was a child. Her parents told her to "suck it up,"
as they couldn't take time off work and she was too young
to stay home alone.

So, she pushed through and went to school feeling like hell. She threw up in front of her class and sat feeling miserable and embarrassed in the nurse's office until her mom arrived to take her home. What's the message here? "Work is more important than the health of your body. Stuff it. Suck it up until you can't."

Many of us also received messages from the media, our families, our culture, etc., telling us that we could only love and accept our body if it looked a certain way and had specific characteristics. If it didn't fit the mold, then we began to feel negative, and started to dislike and even hate our body.

I hit puberty very early. In the third grade, I had to start wearing a bra and in the fifth grade I got my period. Since this was a few years earlier than the norm, I was teased by boys and I felt the scorn of other girls. I hated my body because of this. I remember pushing in my breasts, and for over a year I hid the fact that I had my period from my friends.

We can also become disconnected from our bodies if we had body trauma while growing up, such as physical abuse, sexual abuse, or an accident, to name a few possibilities.

When your body is disfigured in any way by an accident, you not only have the emotional trauma to deal with, but also the physical wounds which others can see, stare at and judge. We feel this, and we often turn the judgement on ourselves.

If you are physically and/or sexually abused, you may feel you are broken, dirty, or bad, and blame your body for what happened.

I was sexually abused by several of my male cousins while growing up. That, plus the teasing that came from an early puberty, definitely made me hate and want to disconnect from my body.

After I was date-raped at the age of 15, I put on 20 pounds in about 60 days. At an unconscious level, I wanted to hide my body and make it seem undesirable, so it wouldn't happen again; then I beat myself up for being fat.

So, unfortunately, being disconnected from your body is the norm. Keep reading to learn how to connect, accept, and understand your body and the messages it is bringing you.

Tips, Tools and Inspired Actions:

Regardless of why you became disconnected from your body, here are some tips and tools to help you begin to accept, connect with, and listen to your body and the messages it is bringing you.

Remember: progress not perfection! Start with the Reflect and Write section, then move to one of the connection practices, then keep doing more until you are using all three daily to support your healing.

Also remember that awareness is the key to changing anything in your life.

Let go of any judgement, and reflect with compassion and curiosity on the following:

1. Rate, on a scale of 1-10, how much you accept your body at this moment. 0 = not at all and 10 = completely accept.

2. Rate, on a scale of 1-10, how much you listen to your body and your feelings vs. how much you ignore or resist them at this time. 0 = not at all and 10 = completely listen.

3. Reflect upon and write about the following questions:

   • How did you see or hear your parents in relation to their bodies and their symptoms or feelings?

   • What body feelings or illnesses do your parents have, or did have in the past?

   • What body feelings or illnesses do you have, or did have in the past?

   • What "messages" did you receive about your body growing up?

- Do you have past body trauma? How is it affecting the way you feel about and listen to your body?

4. Mini-Body Connection Practice: Take five minutes each day to do a body connection check-in, preferably in the morning. Sit or lie in a comfortable position. Close your eyes. Breathe for a few moments. Now notice what feelings are present in your face. Then move to each body area in the following order at your own pace: your scalp, neck, right arm, left arm, chest, belly, pelvis/genitals, upper back, middle back, lower back, buttocks, right leg and foot, left leg and foot.

   Write down the feelings that were present as you checked in. You may also want to look them up in the book *Heal Your Body* by Louise Hay to receive clues on the probable cause (e.g. the areas of your life where you are out of alignment with your divine self).

5. Mini-Feelings Practice: Take five minutes each day to complete the following feelings-related practice:

   Part 1 — Sit or lie in a comfortable position with your eyes closed. Breathe. What feeling or area of your body is speaking the loudest today? Allow yourself to feel and be with that feeling or area for a few moments. Silently ask the feeling or area why it's here…what is it telling or showing you? What does it want you to do? Listen for a few moments.

Part 2 — Find an opposite feeling in the body (example: If you were feeling pain, now find an area that feels comfortable). Notice how and where you feel this opposite feeling in the body. Breathe. Feel this for a few moments.

Part 3 — Move back and forth between the two, feeling one and then feeling the opposite. Go at your own pace, and do this several times.

Part 4 — End by feeling both feelings in your body at the same time.

Part 5 — Write down any messages you received from the feeling or area.

6. Guided Therapeutic Meditation Practice: Find a sample practice at www.tanyapenny.com/cdy. Listen to a guided practice 1-3x/day with:

The Intention to: accept and love your body and to accept, understand and heal the feeling or area of _____ in your body.

Your Heart's Desire in Mind: Say these words: "I am always listening to my body; My body is healthy, whole, and healed; I love and accept my body always."

A Strong Body Connection: Notice what is present in your body during the rotation.

A Focus on Feelings: Choose the feeling or area that is speaking the loudest when you listen to the meditation and identify an opposite to work with (example: pain + comfort).

Self-Connection and Your Body/Feelings:

A Client Connection

Laura's Story

Laura was a college student and a musician with a very busy schedule. She often felt over-whelmed, sometimes lacked confidence, and she was also stressing about finding a job after graduation. She would often wake up anxious, and she struggled with bouts of depression.

Why She Came to See Me

Laura was referred to me by one of her music professors. She was seeking support to heal chronic stomach pain, upper body tension, insomnia, and stress. She wanted to learn ways to stress less, be healthier and feel more balanced and peaceful, no matter what was happening in her life.

How We Worked Together

Laura and I decided that the best way for us to begin working together was through private sessions via phone, since we lived in different states. We met every two or three weeks, and then moved to once a month for the space of a year. We focused on one or two self-connection areas of the Therapeutic Meditation Process each session, and then Laura would practice using her tools between sessions, while also working on the other inspired actions I suggested.

The Issue at the Heart of the Matter:

Over the course of our work together, Laura took time to connect with all parts of herself daily, through reflecting, journaling, and using a guided therapeutic meditation practice. She also used these tools to look at her past to discover what had been causing her to disconnect from her true self.

In reflecting, she realized she had a pattern of "all or nothing," striving for perfection, and she was quick to judge herself. She would fall off the self-care wagon and into the pattern over-doing it when things felt unknown or out of her control. She often felt responsible for helping friends or family members solve their problems, and she unconsciously took on their emotions, trying to help them feel better (so she would feel better).

Laura saw that her unhealthy patterns came from being the oldest child, and from having a mother who was always trying to improve herself, and who strived to be the best. She had a father who lacked confidence and tried to make up for it by working hard. He would also drop everything and do anything for his family — which is great unless it means you are not taking care of your own wants and needs, too. Laura also saw that her stomach pain, anxiety, depression and sleep disturbance were caused by all the worry, striving and stress these unhealthy patterns (and the beliefs that were driving them) were putting on her. They were causing her to fall out of balance and become disconnected from her true self.

I recommended that Laura start feeling and releasing her negative emotions through journaling, and that she use the guided therapeutic meditation practices during the day, and again at bedtime as she was falling asleep.

Also, I suggested she use these tools to work with the beliefs that were causing her to fall into the unhealthy patterns: "I have to be perfect in all areas of her life, I have to work hard to be good enough, I am responsible for others, and I have to do/control to be survive."

We worked on supporting her to plant new beliefs and desires: "I'm good enough without doing anything, I don't have to be perfect, I love and accept myself just as I am, I don't have to work hard to be worthy, I'm not responsible for other people's lives, and I'm always divinely guided and supported." This was all designed to heal these unhealthy patterns and shift her actions.

Laura was able to reign in her inner Superwoman (who caused her to do or work too much), and she developed a daily routine that was more balanced with time to connect with herself.

She practiced just listening to others without taking it on as her responsibility to fix their problems. She would notice sooner when she did fall into these patterns, and she used her tools to shift them to come back into balance again.

Implications and Results

After working with me, Laura's tension in her upper body began to dissolve and, if it came back, she swiftly used her tools to release it. She was feeling less anxious and sleeping better. If she felt depressed, she realized it was because she was likely judging herself for not being perfect and she would switch her self-talk to that of compassion and acceptance. Her emergency room visits for stomach pain stopped. Anytime she felt a twinge, she would use her tools to release the worry and shift the beliefs that were causing it. Overall, Laura was feeling the connection, balance and peace she had always desired, and she now listens to her feelings and emotions and the messages they are bringing her, if they arise.

In Laura's Own Words:

Through my coaching sessions with Tanya and learning the Therapeutic Meditation Process (TMP)®, I have become more aware of my body, emotions and, most importantly, what messages they are bringing me. Before practicing the TMP I was admitted to the emergency room once every couple of months due to severe stomach pain. I would also have to take weeks off from practicing flute due to severe neck, shoulder and arm pain. Thanks to Tanya, I no longer have severe stomach pain, am able to keep my body relaxed using my tools, and I have created balance in my life while having a busy schedule."

- *Laura*

Chapter 7: Your Emotions

You have to feel, understand and release your emotions to fully heal. — Tanya Penny

I have not met one person in my life (yet) who is able to fully acknowledge, accept, feel, release, *and* express all of their emotions with others…in a healthy way.

Being able to do this is critical to our health. Which is why most of us end up with negative feelings (symptoms) in our body, or even a chronic illness. I know that this was one of the reasons I suffered from eating disorders, excess weight, and, eventually, Multiple Sclerosis.

Before we dive into this important topic of emotions, I must clear something up. Many of us use the words "feelings" and "emotions" interchangeably, as though they mean the same thing. When you are working with me, the word "emotions" means: anxious, calm, sad, happy, angry, peaceful, secure, insecure, shame, guilt, love, to name a few. "Feelings" are physical sensations or symptoms in the body (see Chapter 6).

Cool! Now that we got that cleared up, let's go for it… I promise it won't be that bad. ☺

Why is Connecting with Our Emotions Important?

In a nutshell, emotions are a part of you. We don't ever want to reject any part of us. Period. As with any self-connection area, acceptance is key. Emotions are your internal messengers. They are not good or bad, right or wrong. They simply provide you with information, giving you clues about the one or more areas of your life where you might be out of balance. They also show where you are not setting or keeping healthy boundaries with yourself and/or others.

Other than that, there are three primary reasons why you want to learn to deal with your emotions in a healthy way:

1. **In order to have a healthy body.** As mind-body healing philosophy notes, when we do not acknowledge, feel, release or express our emotions in healthy ways, we tend to "stuff" them down inside us so tightly that they might never see the light of day. They then build up inside of us, and, over time, start to show up as negative feelings or symptoms in our body (pain, fatigue, headaches, high blood pressure, etc.). If we still do not get the hint, and we refuse or neglect to deal with our emotions, they will get louder and louder and the symptoms will get increasingly serious, perhaps even turning into a chronic illness, as happened for me. As one of my favorite teachers, Carolyn Myss, says, "You have to feel it to heal it."

2. **In order to receive your guidance.** Your emotions are one of the ways you can receive guidance. They let you know if you are in or out of alignment with your true self – your wants, needs, and desires—in all areas of your life. If you are in the habit of stuffing your emotions, you will not be able to hear the guidance or message they are trying to give you.

3. **In order to feel your positive emotions.** When you cut off your "negative" emotions, you turn down your ability to fully and authentically feel your "positive" emotions, too.
Now, I must add that many people say they feel joyful, peaceful or happy, and perhaps even outwardly appear or act as if they feel that way... but it's usually not authentic. They have brainwashed themselves to believe and act as if they feel that way in order to cope, get by and, in some cases, to actually survive. Many of my clients did not realize they had stuffed so many negative emotions down inside them until we began working together. They had learned it was only okay to act happy, or express happy emotions, when they were growing up. Some even learned to stuff the positive emotions because it made someone else feel worse when they were happy. So, they came to feel and express nothing and always appeared "neutral" or blank.

Why Don't I Feel and Deal with My Emotions?

The Million Dollar Question I often get asked by my clients is *"why* do I stuff my emotions?" The simple answer: You didn't learn how to deal with your emotions (in a healthy way) when you were growing up; you were afraid to feel or express your emotions; OR you were ignored. Here's a little more detail on that topic:

1. **You learned to stuff your emotions.** As we grow up we almost automatically learn to behave according to what we see and/or hear our parents or other adults doing. This will happen unless we become aware of how automatic this is, and unless we consciously choose to learn to do things differently when we become an adult. Like me and most of my clients, one or both of your parents likely did not model healthy ways of dealing with their emotions. I saw my mom stuff her "negative" emotions with food, TV-watching, and shopping. I saw my dad escape his "negative" emotions through drinking, drugs, watching TV or leaving and running away.

    From a young age, I stuffed my negative emotions of loneliness, anger, sadness, insecurity and self-hatred down inside me by overeating. In my teen years, I moved into drinking, drugs and starving myself. Through college and into my late 20s and early 30s, I continued with drinking, and I added binging and purging, sex, over-exercising and — my favorite — over-achieving.

Here are a few more ways you might be stuffing your emotions: gambling, over-working, over sleeping, trying to control other people or situations, worrying or staying busy, busy, busy (so that you are too busy to feel anything).

We are not blaming our parents. They were doing the best that they could, as they probably didn't have great role models growing up, either. My mother learned to eat from her mother, and my dad learned to drink from his father, etc. The emotional stuffing cycle continued on down the line... until now. It can stop with me and you.

2. **You were afraid to feel or express your emotions.** Perhaps you were also taught to stuff your emotions out of fear—fear of someone yelling, criticizing or embarrassing you, OR maybe you were afraid you would cause someone else to get upset, which would create more conflict...or worse.

   When our parents (or other adults) are not capable of dealing with their own emotions, then they are also usually not capable of dealing with ours or anyone else's. Growing up, I saw that when my mom tried to express her emotions to my dad, especially sadness, he would get angry and even throw things sometimes. Of course, seeing this, I took on the belief or story that "it was not safe" to express my emotions to him. And, when I tried to express "negative" emotions to my mom, she would often get upset and cry. I didn't want to make her upset and sad, so I stopped expressing how I truly felt to her, too.

Perhaps you also fear feeling your negative or painful emotions because you don't think you can handle the pain, or maybe you are afraid of getting stuck in it…forever. The truth is, as a child you were not able to handle painful emotions on your own, and you needed an adult's support to do so. Most of us did not have parents who could handle their own painful emotions, so they could not support or teach us to feel ours. You will learn how to do this below by working with opposites, feeling an emotion for a few moments, and then its opposite. This will help you to stop pushing them away, and you won't get stuck in them, either. This is important, as you can't hear your emotion's message if you push it away, and you can't take action on the message if you are stuck in it.

3. **You were ignored, or a parent was not present.** Maybe you did try to express your emotions, but it fell on deaf ears. Your mom or dad might have been too busy, distracted by work or your siblings, and maybe they ignored you. So, again, you stopped, because you started to think, "What's the use?" Or maybe you thought, "They must not care anyway," or "What I feel isn't important." Perhaps like some of my clients, you grew up living with only one parent. If or when you did see the other parent, you wanted to be "good," so you didn't share

anything negative or "bad" with them and spoil your time together.

4. **You "take on" or manage other people's emotions.** Perhaps while growing up, you were conditioned to deal with or fix other people's emotions. And you continue to do this as an adult with your birth family, spouse, children, friends, etc. It's hard to feel and deal with your own emotions when you are busy trying to manage or tend to someone else's, especially if you are doing it to receive love, safety, etc. When we take on a role or "pattern" as children, we often continue repeating it in adulthood until we become aware of it, and can then consciously decide to change it.

Again, we are not here to blame anyone, or make them wrong or bad. Our parents (or other adults who raised or taught us in childhood) were doing their best at the time, and so were we. We still all are. And awareness is the key to changing anything in our lives. So, it's important to see why and how we started stuffing our emotions in the first place. Plus, it helps us to have compassion for ourselves, our parents, and our stuffing patterns. This is so much healthier than beating ourselves up about them.

Now that you have that awareness and compassion, let's begin to learn new, healthy ways to acknowledge, feel, release and express your emotions.

Tips, Tools and Inspired Actions:

Since we have become accustomed to stuffing and avoiding our emotions, this next part might feel uncomfortable, or even scary. Again, I have been there… and I am still living! The following are tools I have personally used, and I've taught hundreds of other people to use them, too. Remember that awareness is the key to changing anything in your life. Let go of any judgement and reflect with compassion and curiosity on the following.

1. Rate, on a scale of 1-10, how much you acknowledge, feel, and release your emotions in a healthy way, at this moment. 0 = not at all. 10 = completely, deeply true.

2. Reflect and write on the following questions:

   - How did you see or hear your parents deal with their emotions growing up?

   - Which emotions were okay to feel or express and which were not okay?

   - What stuffing technique(s) did they use?

   - What stuffing techniques do you use? Now or in the past? Which emotions do you try to stuff?

3. Journal. Take 1-5 minutes each day to write about or journal the emotions you are experiencing and why (what are the situations that create an emotional response?). If you are not sure why you feel an emotion, ask "Is this my emotion or someone else's?" If guidance says "mine," then ask which situation, belief or thought is causing it. If guidance says "someone else's," see below. Ask your emotion what it is telling or showing you, or what it is asking you to do. Speak up and express something to someone? Say "no" or set a boundary?

4. Mini-Emotions Practice.

   Part 1: Take a few moments. Close your eyes. Breathe. Think about or visualize a situation from your journal, or an event that has just occurred. Allow yourself to feel the emotion that comes up. Breathe. Notice how and where you feel it in your body, and place your hand where you feel it. Tell yourself it is safe and okay to feel it. Continue to feel and breathe. Ask your emotion what it is telling you, showing you, or asking you to do. Speak up and express something to someone? Say "no," or set a boundary?

   Part 2: Choose an opposite emotion. Close your eyes and remember a time when you were experiencing this emotion. (Example: If you were feeling sad, perhaps now choose to feel happy). Notice how or where you feel this opposite emotion in your body. Breathe. Stay here as long as you like.

Part 3: Move back and forth between your two emotions, feeling one and then feeling the opposite. Go at your own pace, and do this several times (with your eyes closed). End by visualizing yourself holding both emotions, one in each hand.

5. Guided Therapeutic Meditation Practice. Listen to a guided TMP practice 1-3x/day to acknowledge, feel, understand and release your emotions. Always work with the emotion that is speaking the loudest each time. Find a sample practice at www.tanyapenny.com/cdy, and set some intentions to:

- Feel and release your emotion of _____ (fill in the blank).

- Receive clarity on what the emotion is showing or asking you. Use an emotion that is speaking the loudest each time.

- Release someone else's emotion from your energy fields.

Self-Connection and Your Emotions:

A Client Connection

Angela's Story

Angela had recently been told she had "possible" Multiple Sclerosis and she was seeking to decrease and heal her symptoms of fatigue, numbness, weakness, and anxiety, using alternative healing methods. She had some long-standing issues with her body image that she wanted to shift, and she also wanted support with the grief she was feeling, in the wake of her father's recent passing.

Why She Came to See Me

Angela found me by coming to a free live community class I was hosting. She was a stay-at-home mother with a young son and she wanted to be as healthy as possible, so she could continue to take care of him.

How We Worked Together

Angela and I decided that best way for us to work together was through private sessions in person and we saw each other twice a month for several months. We focused on one or two self-connection areas of the Therapeutic Meditation Process each session, and then Angela would practice using her tools between sessions, while also working on the other inspired actions I suggested.

The Issue at the Heart of the Matter:

Over the course of our time together, Angela began connecting with all parts of herself daily through reflecting, journaling, and using guided therapeutic meditation practices. She also used her tools to reflect on her past to see how it might have contributed to her health issues. In reflecting, she saw that she was the oldest child in her family and she had taken on the role of caregiver for herself and her younger brother because her parents were often not physically or emotionally present. This created unhealthy "Superwoman" and perfection patterns where she believed she was responsible for others, had to do it all, alone, perfectly, to survive.

Angela realized that these patterns were still running her today. She tried to be the perfect mom and wife, she took care of the household, and she rarely asked for support from her husband. She didn't take much time to care for herself. She also saw how her body image issues had to do with trying to be perfect. All of this caused her to feel a lot of anxiety and overwhelm. Angela was also carrying grief and guilt from her father's recent death. She thought that if she had done more, or done things differently, he might be alive today. Again, her inner "Superwoman" was saying she was responsible for what happened to others.

Angela's negative emotions were creating the symptoms she was experiencing in her body as she didn't know how to feel and release them in healthy ways. She had only learned how to stuff them, as her parents had.

Angela used the Therapeutic Meditation Process to help her to acknowledge, feel and release her negative emotions in healthy ways. She took time daily to connect and journal about which emotions were present for her.

She would then also use the mini-emotions practice or a guided therapeutic meditation practice to help her feel and release the emotions.

Angela also used her tools to shift the beliefs that were keeping her stuck in the unhealthy patterns of perfection and the Superwoman Syndrome: "I have to do it all, alone, I have to do it perfectly, I'm responsible for others' lives, I can't ask for support." The goal was to plant new beliefs and desires: "I don't have to be perfect, I feel and release my emotions in healthy ways, I can ask for and receive support, I'm not responsible for the lives of others."

Angela started to ask for support. She enrolled her son in a child-care program several times a week, so she could take time to connect with herself, rest and heal. She realized that she also had a passion for yoga and, after her health returned, she decided to start yoga teacher training.

Implications and Results

After working together for a year, Angela's numbness, weakness and fatigue dissolved. She developed a healthier relationship with her body and took time to nurture it daily.

She uses a guided therapeutic meditation practice before picking her son up from childcare, so she can feel rested and relaxed. She feels she now has a healthy balance of doing for others and doing for herself. She is now a yoga teacher who supports others to take time to connect with themselves as well.

In Angela's Own Words:

Since Tanya and I have been coaching together, my life has changed in so many positive ways.

I began working with Tanya in the midst of a chronic health diagnosis and the recent passing of my father.

Tanya taught me how to feel and heal the physical and emotional pain (fear, grief, and guilt) that were causing my negative body symptoms.

I also had longstanding body image and weight issues. I am learning to accept myself just as I am, and to celebrate and nurture my body, using her Therapeutic Meditation Process (TMP). No longer do I allow the scale to dictate how I feel about myself, or what kind of day I will have.

Tanya has taught me how to connect with myself and make me a priority. I even got the courage to follow my heart and become a yoga teacher! I highly recommend coaching with Tanya Penny: her work is life changing!

– Angela

Chapter 8: Your Beliefs

Whatever you believe, you will always be right, and you will make it true. — Tanya Penny

Your beliefs determine the way you feel and behave, and they also determine what you attract into your life.

Your beliefs can hold you back from pursuing your goals — and even make you sick — or they can support you to heal and co-create the life of your dreams.

This chapter focuses on what beliefs are, where they come from, and why it's important to discover the beliefs you hold. It also shares tips and tools to help you shift any beliefs that are self-limiting, causing a chronic illness, or keeping you from enjoying abundance in all areas of your life.

When I was healing from Multiple Sclerosis, I stumbled onto the concept that beliefs were much more important than I had previously thought. That was incredibly fortunate for me because otherwise I might be confined to a wheelchair today, rather than living an energetic life that sees me running and hiking in the full appreciation of what it means to be "MS-free." And I would only possibly be in that wheelchair if I had believed what the doctors had told me about MS being progressive and incurable.

If you don't believe what you are reading, then keep reading, and let's see if I can change your belief by the end of the chapter!

What Are Beliefs and Where Do They Come From?

A belief is a thought you keep thinking, over and over. Beliefs can be positive, supporting us to attract what our soul truly desires, or negative, self-limiting, and holding us back from what we truly want and deserve. A thought creates a neural pathway in the brain.

The more you think the thought, the deeper the groove it creates in your brain. This makes it easier for your brain to think that thought, but it also makes it more difficult for you to shift and think a different thought, if you decide you want to.

The beliefs you hold often come from what you have experienced in life, but they may also come from what you were told, heard or saw while growing up in the company of your family, culture or society, religion, media, and peers. Even as adults, we can take on new beliefs based on the opinions of those around us.

Growing up, I saw and heard my mom do things just to please other people, even if she really didn't want to do them. This often meant she didn't take time to nurture and care for herself in ways that would make her happy.

I realized when I was diagnosed with Multiple Sclerosis, that I also had a hard time saying no, and I did a lot of things I didn't want to do because I took on the belief that "I had to please others," and "I couldn't say no."

We are often not aware or conscious of many of the beliefs we hold. Most of us don't realize what we believe until we start down a path of personal growth and healing. That's often when we recognize that we have beliefs, and that we can choose to shift the ones that are not in alignment with what we desire in the seven life areas: self, health, spirituality, love and relationships, passions, purpose and career, and money and material possessions.

Many of our beliefs have been coping mechanisms that we took on at a young age because we believed they would keep us safe and secure, and help us survive in the world. We also thought they would help us earn praise, love or money. Our beliefs may or may not have worked for us then, and even those that brought positive results when we were children are likely not true or not "working" for us anymore.

Importance of Discovering and Shifting Your Beliefs

If you are not happy about a certain area of your life, or have been trying to make changes but can't seem to "make it happen," you are likely being sabotaged by your beliefs. Perhaps you want to exercise or meditate every day but can't seem to "make the time" to actually do it. You might be holding the belief that "I have to put work or others first," or "Exercise or meditation is too hard," or "If I don't do it for X minutes, it's not worth it."

Maybe you want to switch jobs or careers. If you're holding the belief that "I'm not smart enough or good enough to do 'X,'" or "I'll fail or make a mistake," then you are limiting your chances of success. Many of our beliefs cause stress, anxiety, and depression. They can also cause us to behave in ways that are making us sick or keeping us from fully healing.

I realized that I had taken on the belief that "I have to do everything perfectly" as a result of my father's way of being in the world, and that it was causing me a lot of anxiety. When I didn't do something "perfectly," I would beat up on myself and spin into depression.

I also held the belief that "I'm not good enough," so I tried to prove I was "good enough" by over-working and over-doing things personally and professionally. The act of push, push, pushing myself mentally and physically wore me down, and I believe that over time it became one of the root causes of my Multiple Sclerosis diagnosis.

Discover Your Beliefs

If you want to experience the relief that comes from shifting your beliefs onto a more productive neural pathway, you will first want to spend some time discovering what beliefs you might be holding that are keeping you unhappy, stuck or sick: we can't change anything about which we are unaware. If that resonates with you, then you will want to begin using some of the shifting tools listed below *daily*. This will allow you to begin changing the self-limiting beliefs you discover through the reflection and writing process. Remember, you have likely been holding onto any self-limiting beliefs you uncover for a long time. It may take some time to plant the seeds of new ones and allow them to flourish. Curiosity, patience, compassion, and practice will support you in the shifting process.

Take a look at your beliefs in all seven life areas: self, health, spirituality, love and relationships, passions, purpose and career, and money and material possessions. Ask yourself the following questions, and write down your answers:

1. What is your current reality for each area? Write down what you are not happy with, or don't like, for each category.

2. Reflect on what you remember hearing or seeing while growing up for each area and write it down.

3. Given what you found in #1 and #2 above, list the beliefs you might be holding. Then write down an opposite, or potential new truth for each (even if you don't fully believe it right now).

Examples:

Self

"I'm not good enough" vs. "I am worthwhile, lovable, and perfect just as I am"

"My needs, emotions, and desires aren't important" vs. "I am important"

"I'm a disappointment, and a failure" vs. "I'm good enough just as I am"

"I can't trust myself" vs. "I am trustworthy and following my guidance"

"I am powerless and stuck" vs. "I have choices"

Spirituality

"I'm not safe or supported" vs. "I am always safe, loved, and supported"

"I'm all alone, and have to figure out and do everything by myself" vs. "I'm always guided and supported" "I can't trust something bigger than me" vs. "I am trusting in my 'Something Bigger'" (SB) more every day" "I will be punished if I don't do _____" vs. "My SB loves and supports me unconditionally"

Health

"I'll never heal" vs. "I am healing more everyday"

"I'm not healing fast enough" vs. "I am healing in divine time"
"Everyone in my family suffers from _____" vs. "I can and will break the family tradition of _____."

Love and Relationships

"My family should love and accept me" vs. "I love and accept me"

"I have to please everyone and make them happy" vs. "I need to make me happy"

"I will always be rejected, hurt or abandoned" vs. "I attract people who honor and love me for me"

"I should be able to do it all" vs. "It's necessary to ask for support"

Money and Material Possessions

"I will never have enough money" vs. "I always have an abundance of money"

"I have to work hard to make money" vs. "I am receiving money with ease"

"Money is dirty, evil and causes conflict" vs. "Money is good, easy and I do good things with it."

Passions

"It's selfish to make time for me" vs. "It's necessary for my health and happiness to make time for what I love"

"My desires aren't important" vs. "My passions are very important to my health and well-being"

"I don't have money to pursue my passions" vs. "My passions are important to save for, and give to"

Purpose and Career

"I'll never find my purpose" vs. "I am already living my purpose, and it will continue to unfold in divine time"

"I'll make mistakes and fail" vs. "There are no mistakes or failures, just learning opportunities that allow me to grow"

"I can't make money doing what I love" vs. "I am easily receiving money doing what I love"

Note: Pay attention when the words "should," "have to," or "supposed to" come into your mind or out of your mouth. These are red flags indicating that a belief is present that you may need to look at and decide to shift.

Tips, Tools and Inspired Actions:

The following will support you to re-program the beliefs that are holding you back, and it will allow you to plant seeds for, and integrate, the beliefs with which you would like to replace them.

Remember, no belief you hold is "bad," it just might not be serving you at this time. You desire to shift it, so you can heal and have the life you truly desire.

As you use these tools over time, your new reality will continue to unfold.:

1. Journal.

   - Take a few minutes each morning to look at the list of beliefs that have been holding you back, and making you sick. Continued awareness of these is key. At the end of the day, reflect on any that affected you, or held you back, etc., bringing a sense of compassion and curiosity to your reflection.

   - Take a few minutes each morning and evening to write and affirm (out loud or silently) your new beliefs or truths in each life area. It is helpful to also visualize them as you affirm them.

2. Write your new beliefs or truths on post-it notes, or with dry-erase marker on mirrors, even schedule them as events in your calendar. The more you focus on them, the more you plant the seeds and integrate them as your truths, and your daily desired actions will follow suit.

3. Mini Beliefs Practice:

   Part 1: Chose a self-limiting belief. Close your eyes and affirm it. Notice what feelings, emotions, images or memories arise when you do this. Open your eyes and write down anything you feel guided to write.

Part 2: Choose an opposite belief or truth. Close your eyes and affirm it. Notice what feelings, emotions, images or memories arise when you do this. Open your eyes and write down anything you feel guided to write.

Part 3: Visualize yourself holding both beliefs, one in each hand, having compassion and acceptance for both. End by affirming the belief that you would like to continue to cultivate and integrate as your truth.

4. Guided Therapeutic Meditation Practice: You can find a helpful, sample guided practice at www.tanyapenny.com/cdy. Listen to a guided therapeutic meditation practice 1-3x/day to plant the seeds for what you desire, and to feel, understand, and release the feelings and emotions caused by the limiting beliefs. This will also support you to shift your limiting beliefs and plant the seeds for your new beliefs.

Self-Connection and Your Beliefs:

A Client Connection

Leda's Story

About seven years ago, Leda thought she had the flu, then ended up with 14 months of headaches, muscle spasms, muscle tics, visual disturbances, extreme fatigue, joint pains, brain fog, and all kinds of other unexplained weirdness. She recovered to about 80% of where she had been previously, but she was still was struggling.

Why She Came to See Me

Leda came through my virtual door by word-of-mouth. A woman she worked with had had great success in working with me to heal her anxiety, adrenal burnout and fatigue, and now Leda wanted my support. She was looking for assistance with healing chronic migraines, fatigue, brain fog, stomach issues, sleep disturbance and low back pain that she had been experiencing for 14 years. She was in an unfulfilling relationship with her partner of 20 years. His drinking had become a problem and he didn't want to connect with her emotionally or physically — they hadn't had sex for 12 years. She stayed in the marriage hoping he would eventually get help and that things would change.

117

Exercising consistently had become very difficult, even though Leda had previously been a triathlete. Leda was able to exercise well some days, but on others it would throw her into a mini-relapse of all her negative symptoms. She was also having trouble managing the "administrative" details of life, like paying bills, making medical appointments, etc. Her inability to focus and manage tasks was beginning to affect her performance at work as well.

How We Worked Together

Given the numerous issues and the number of areas of her life that Leda wanted to heal, I recommended working together in my Vibrant Body & Abundant Life Mastery program, which included private sessions with me via phone, listening to audio lessons and embracing the guided therapeutic meditation practices on my 10 Vibrant Body & Abundant Life Blueprint Keys program. The program also invited her to attend the virtual group classes I hold each month, so she could connect with, and receive support from, others going through similar healing experiences.

The Issue at the Heart of the Matter

Leda agreed she had become disconnected from who she was and what she really wanted in her life. Over the course of our time together, I asked Leda to take time to connect with herself daily through reflecting, writing exercises, and using guided therapeutic meditation practices. She used these tools to ask her body what messages it was trying to give her, determine what emotions she was experiencing, and what she really desired in all areas of her life, and also to uncover the limiting beliefs that arose when she connected with these parts of herself.

Leda discovered many things through this self-connection process. She realized she didn't like to be alone or spend time alone with herself, which was why she stayed in her marriage and filled her social schedule: that meant that there was little time available for her to be and feel alone.

She also remained in an unfulfilling relationship because she believed, on a deep level, that she didn't deserve better, and that she wasn't lovable or worthy, so she should just take what she could get in a partner.

Her job was not feeding her soul and she over-worked at it because she was trying to prove her worthiness; her marital unhappiness meant she escaped through working.

This core belief of "I'm not lovable, wanted or worthy" kept her stuck in these unhealthy patterns and situations. This belief came from her experience of having been giving up for adoption when she was born.

Even though she was adopted by a wonderful family, she felt different, and as though she wasn't fully accepted for who she was. Leda worked on shifting this limiting belief both consciously and subconsciously through daily writing exercises, guided therapeutic meditation practices and taking actions that were in alignment with the truth "I am always lovable, worthy just being my true self."

Implications and Results

After a few months of working together, Leda decided that she was going to move out of her house and separate from her partner. She cut back on the hours she was working, and the number of social gatherings she attended, and made more time to connect with herself.

She rested instead of being stuck in a trajectory of "do, go, do."

As she made these changes, all of her symptoms started to decrease.

Today, Leda is divorced and happily dating a variety of men. She is unwilling to settle for less than what she deserves and desires. She has control over her financial situation and she has her organizational skills back.

She did gradually leave her job, and she started a business that gives her the flexibility and income she desires.

She is now pursuing the goal of becoming a coach to support women who have struggled with the same things she did.

And her health? Leda no longer has brain fog, she sleeps well most nights, and her fatigue is gone.

The migraines happen much less often and with much less intensity than they used to, and the same is true of her back pain.

When things do flare up, she is able to use her self-connection tools, hear the messages her body is bringing her, and make the needed changes in her life; then the problems dissolve.

Her stomach issues are much less severe, and she is weaning herself off her medications for them even as I write this.

In Leda's Own Words:

Working with Tanya has helped me transform my life in multiple ways. Tanya's blend of practicality, compassion, smarts, spirituality, and humor helped me overcome my fears and get out of some rough places.

In the last 13 months, I've gotten clear about what I want and need in my life. I had the courage to leave a marriage that was no longer working for me, I changed my tendency to overwork in a job that doesn't inspire me, I got a handle on my money issues, I started planning a new career, and I boosted my health.

I have a lot more trust and confidence in myself, and I'm able to communicate my feelings and my needs.

I take better care of myself physically and mentally, realizing for the first time in my life that it's not selfish to put my needs first.

I don't beat myself up anymore, either. I feel confident that I'm creating a kick-ass life for myself. I'm in a relationship with a guy who gets me, loves me, supports me, and is incredibly fun. I feel happy and open to the world again.

When I do feel sad, scared, or any other negative emotion, I now have the tools to figure out the root cause and a way to feel it and move forward. Tanya's 1:1 support as well as the "Vibrant Body & Abundant Life" community has been absolutely vital for me in making these huge positive transitions in my life.

- Leda

Chapter 9: Something Bigger

We are powerful co-creators, always connected to and guided by Something Bigger. — Tanya Penny

If you had told me five years ago that I would be writing and teaching about spirituality or "Something Bigger," I would have laughed in your face. And yet, here I am. Life sure can throw us funny surprises!

In a nutshell, I believe we were all created by something. (And not just our parents, ha-ha!). You might call this Something Bigger (SB) or give it a name like God, Universe, Source, Yahweh, Allah, Creator, Nature, My Angels and Guides, and so on.

We are always connected to and guided by this Something Bigger (even if we think we are not). But we can choose to disconnect or disbelieve for many reasons, some of which I will describe below.

In this chapter I'll be sharing with you my personal journey back to trusting in SB, plus providing some tips and tools you can use to re-connect and trust on a deeper level. Before we continue, however, I feel it's important to talk about spirituality and religion. Religion and spirituality aren't necessarily the same thing, although they can be.

123

I don't follow any religion at this time in my life, yet I believe in Something Bigger. My name for my SB is my "Higher Levels."

You don't have to be a part of a religion to be spiritual or to believe in Something Bigger. But you might express your spirituality through a religious philosophy.

Wherever you find yourself today is okay. This chapter will support you to more deeply connect and trust in whatever way is important for you.

Why Connecting With Something Bigger is Important

It can be very mentally, physically and emotionally stressful to either cut off your connection to your SB, or to not believe in its existence. It can also cause anxiety, depression, and other illnesses.

We can become overwhelmed by life when we think we have to figure everything out alone, and then get it all done alone.

We can also become stuck in the vicious "struggle and survival" cycle that causes us to work too hard, try to *make* things happen, or control everything.

When we believe in, are connected to, and fully trust our SB, by contrast, we feel more relaxed, peaceful, and safe. We face life challenges with more ease and grace.

We make life decisions based on our SB's guidance, instead of through ego-related fear and what others tell us to do.

124

Why We Disconnect or Don't Trust Something Bigger

There are many reasons why we disconnect, don't believe, or don't fully trust SB. Let me share a few of the biggies with you:

1. **Family and Religion.** Maybe you grew up with a religion that didn't resonate with you, or it put a bad taste in your mouth. So, you decided to leave it, and you never replaced it with anything else.

   I had this experience. I grew up Catholic and knew from a young age that this God with lots of rules and judgement wasn't someone I wanted in my life. But I was forced to go to church until I turned 18. After that, I never looked back. I didn't realize at the time that I could explore other religions, or that I could just forget religion and still be spiritual, that I could believe in SB. It wasn't until I was diagnosed with Multiple Sclerosis (MS), and started searching for all that could help me to fully heal, that I started to connect with SB again.

   Maybe you are still practicing a religion that doesn't really resonate with you because you feel pressured by your family to do so. Trust me, this will also keep you from fully connecting and trusting in SB. I've also known clients who didn't grow up with a family that believed in, or practiced any religion or spirituality, and they were never encouraged to explore it on their own. So, they didn't.

2. **Negative Past Experiences and Trauma.** If you had a negative past experience or trauma (and who hasn't?) you may believe there must not be a SB watching your back, or those bad things wouldn't have happened. Or, if there is SB, you certainly can't rely on it, or trust it.

   I had many negative past experiences and abuse growing up. So, I fell into this category, too. And what about all the "bad" things that happen in the world? They make it even harder to believe there is Something Bigger that is taking care of us: if it exists, why is it just standing by, letting all this stuff happen, or worse, *making* it happen?

3. **Busy Bee.** Perhaps you, like most, are caught up in the pattern of what I call Superwoman (or Superman) Syndrome. You are always on the go, go, go and always do, do, doing something — hitting deadlines at work, taking care of your family, heading out to social engagements, and all those other things you have crammed on to your to-do list and in to your schedule.

   If this is you, how on Earth do you make time to connect with your SB? Perhaps you've cut the connection time short, spending a few minutes praying in the morning, or at night before you go to bed. Maybe you've whittled it down to once a week. Or simply stopped making time to connect with your SB at all, saying you'll do it when things slow down a bit in your life.

4. **Not Special Enough or Good Enough.** Many religions teach that you need a middle man, someone who can connect you to SB because you aren't special enough to connect directly. Some of us compound that belief system with our embrace of the "not good enough" syndrome. We think that we are not worthy enough to directly connect with SB or, if we try, they wouldn't listen or help us anyway.

5. **Control and Fear.** Many of us are control queens (or kings). Why on Earth would we fully trust in SB? We must take matters into our own hands and make shit happen in order to get what we want, in order to survive. If you experienced past trauma, you probably fall into this category as well. Of *course* you want to try and control everything: you want to make sure the trauma doesn't happen again.

   Trusting and acting on our guidance from SB can be scary stuff. It might mean that if we hear and follow its guidance, we could lose love, approval, or money. We could cause conflict, be left alone in the world, or even get physically hurt. That is why some of us don't want to connect more deeply at all. They think (consciously or not) that it's better not to connect at all so they don't even have to hear the guidance in the first place. It's way too risky.

Truths About Connecting with Something Bigger

- You are always connected to SB, whether you believe it, feel it or not.

- You are always loved, guided, and supported by your SB, no matter what you do or don't do.

- Something Bigger is not making bad things happen. As souls, we have chosen to have certain experiences in this lifetime, to know what it feels like, to wake us up, and to evolve. You may not know or understand why something happened in your life until months or years pass, or even until you die.

- Guidance from your SB often won't make sense, seem rational or logical, or even be understood or meet with the approval of others.

- You will likely be given guidance one small bit or step at a time.

- Let go of the idea that you need a guarantee or expected outcome before you can follow your guidance. There is no such thing. Only our SB sees the big picture and even that can shift, since we still all have free will and can choose to do what we please. So, take the action, and then get out of the way…and trust.

- Let go of needing someone else's approval before you follow your divine guidance. This is your path. Not theirs. The people who truly love you will continue to love you, no matter what you do.

- There are no mistakes or failures. You may be guided to do something that doesn't "work out" because it wasn't meant to. You were meant to learn or grow from the experience.

Tips, Tools and Inspired Actions:

I recommend carving out some time daily (15-30 minutes) to read, move through, and use the tools listed below. Remember: progress not perfection. Small changes daily create big shifts and healing over time.

1. Rate, on a scale of 1-10, how much you believe in, connect with, and trust your SB at this moment. You may want to rate all three areas separately, or together. It's up to you. 0 = not at all. 10 = completely, deeply connected.

2. Reflect / write on the following questions: Remember that awareness is the key to changing anything in your life. Let go of any judgement you have, and reflect with compassion and curiosity on the following:

- Do you believe in Something Bigger now? If not, why not? If yes, what do you call it?

- How often do you connect with it? And how do you connect?

- Growing up, what did you hear, see or learn about religion, spirituality, or SB?

- Did you experience any trauma or other negative experiences in your past that affect your belief and trust in SB?

- What keeps you from connecting with, and fully trusting your SB? (See the five biggies above.)

- Given all you've learned in this chapter, and looking at your answers to the reflection questions above, what beliefs might you hold that are keeping you from believing in, connecting with and fully trusting your SB? Write them down. Then write an opposite possible truth for each. You may want to use the examples below.

Examples:

➢ "I don't want to connect with SB, it makes me feel bad or shameful" vs. "My SB is kind, loving, and accepting of me"

➢ "I can't trust SB. It lets bad things happen to me and the world" vs. "I can trust SB, and know all that happens is for the highest good of all"

➢ "I can't connect, I'm not good or special enough" vs. "I am always good enough, and I am connected, and guided, by SB"

➢ "If I follow my SB guidance I'll lose love, money, or cause conflict" vs. "I follow my guidance, knowing that I'm always supported, no matter what happens"

3   Mini-Connection Practice. Once each day (or several times a day), lie or sit in a comfortable position, close your eyes, and breathe for 1-5 minutes. Once you feel grounded, pray or speak to your SB silently (or aloud). Tell it how you are feeling, ask a question, ask for courage or strength, and then listen or feel for answers. When you feel complete, slowly come back to a state of awareness by gently moving different parts of your body and opening your eyes. Write down what you experienced or received. Remember: we all get our guidance in different ways, and it comes in divine time, not our time. Our fears can block us from receiving it (See how to shift those below).

4   Guided Therapeutic Meditation Practice. Listen to a guided TMP 1-3x/day. (You can find a sample practice at www.tanyapenny.com/cdy .) During this practice:

- Set 1-2 intentions to: feel and release fear, connect with SB, know greater trust or courage, release any beliefs that are holding you back from connecting with and/or following your SB guidance, or ask for clarity on a problem or situation.

- Affirm a Heart's Desire related to connecting with and/or trusting your SB guidance. Examples:
  I'm making time to connect and listen to my SB each day; I'm always loved, guided and supported by my SB; I'm always trusting and following my SB guidance

- Work with a belief and its opposite truth (see above reflect and write questions #1).

5.   Focus. Write your Desires and opposite positive beliefs related to SB on a mirror with a dry erase marker, set these statements as screensavers on your phone or computer, and write them on post it notes to place around your home, office and car. What you focus on continues to nourish the new seeds you have planted, and assist them to grow.

6   Daily Journal. Take 1-5 minutes to:

- Write your problems, questions, etc. in your journal each morning and ask your SB to give you answers or insight. Tell it you are open to receiving it all day long.

- Write your SB beliefs and then the positive opposites/truths (see above reflect and write questions #1) each morning.

- Write down your fears, worries, and concerns before bed every night and ask your Something Bigger to take care of them for you while you sleep.

Self-Connection and Something Bigger:

A Client Connection

Kendall's Story

Kendall had experienced anxiety most of her life, but noticed that it worsened during graduate school and then continued at that level after. She was aware that she had a tendency to stress and worry a lot about her job and other aspects of her life. This caused her to push herself too hard mentally, and physically do too much.

Why She Came to See Me

Kendall came through my virtual door by word of mouth. She was looking for support to heal her anxiety, panic, adrenal burnout, fatigue, and sleep disturbance. She wanted to feel more peaceful, relaxed and energized, and have a more balanced schedule and life before she became a parent.

How We Worked Together

Kendall and I decided that the best way for us to begin working together was in private sessions via phone each month. We focused on one or two Self-Connection Areas of the Therapeutic Meditation Process each session, and then she would practice using her tools between sessions while also working on the other inspired actions I suggested. Later, she also joined the Vibrant Body & Abundant Life Mastery program that included listening to audio lessons and using the guided therapeutic meditation practices on the 10 Vibrant Body & Abundant Life Blueprint Keys.

After a year or so, Kendall felt she was in a really good place and decided to take a break from working together. About a year after that, she reached out again for a "tune-up." She needed support with being a new mother, dealing with overwhelm, fatigue, and work/life balance. We again decided that private sessions combined with the group program, was best for her. This time she also enjoyed interacting in the private FB group to connect with and receive support from others going through similar healing experiences.

The Issue at the Heart of the Matter

Kendall agreed that her fear of not being good enough, and her belief she was responsible for everything, and always had to do more, caused her to feel a lot of anxiety. This also caused her a lot of mental stress and resulted in her working too much. This, in turn, caused her to become disconnected from her true self.

Over the course of our time together, I asked Kendall to take time to connect with all parts of herself daily through reflecting/journaling and guided therapeutic meditation practices during her lunch break and again at bedtime as she fell asleep. She used these tools to get in touch with the messages her body was giving her, help her to feel and release her emotions, and experience more energy. They also helped her to shift the limiting beliefs that were causing her to get stuck in patterns of doing and working too much, and examine what past experiences might have contributed to these beliefs and patterns. Finally, the tools helped her connect with her Something Bigger so she didn't feel the stress of everything being all on her.

Kendall discovered many things through using the self-connection process and tools daily. In reflecting on her past, she saw how the patterns of perfection and pretending to be Superwoman were conditioned in her, so she could survive. Her mother had been diagnosed with cancer when Kendall had been five years old. Kendall had been pretty much on her own, as her mother was sick in bed most of the time, and depressed, and her father worked a lot.

Kendall's mom did eventually heal from the cancer, and, once she did, she adopted three more children over several years. Kendall's parents divorced, and her mom became a single parent spreading herself too thin. When Kendall did express her needs, her mom would often fly off the handle. When Kendall was 14, her mother lost it and kicked her out of the house for asking her to take her on some errands.

Given her past experiences, Kendall saw how she could easily take on the beliefs that "I am all on my own, I have to do it all alone to survive, I have to do it right to make my mom happy and save her, and I have to be perfect and not ask for too much, so I can survive." She also had the model of her dad working a lot, which fueled her "Superwoman" pattern even more.

One of the self-connection areas that Kendall and I worked on a lot was Connecting and Trusting Something Bigger. This was important given her beliefs that she was all alone, had to do everything herself to survive, and felt responsible for everything. To support her to believe in, connect with, and trust Something Bigger, she made time daily to pray and write to her Something Bigger. She used the guided therapeutic meditation practices, and took actions that were in alignment with the truth "I'm always divinely supported and cared for."

Implications and Results

After a few months of working together, Kendall began to feel less anxiety and was able to reign in her "Superwoman," set boundaries at work, and work less. She took her lunch breaks to rest, and connect with herself and Something Bigger. As she made these changes, her energy started to return, she slept better, and she felt more peaceful and relaxed.

Today, Kendall is a proud mother (with one more on the way). Her perfection pattern started to return when she became a new mom, but she was able to see it and use her tools to shift it into a healthy place again. She has good work/life balance, asks for more support when needed, and continues to set healthy boundaries at work and in her social life.

Kendall's Something Bigger guidance is nudging her to find a new career. Kendall is looking as she is guided, trusting that it will all happen in divine time. When challenging things come up, she is able to stay calm, and connected to herself and Something Bigger. This helps her to trust all will be okay, and to ride the waves of certainty with more ease and peace.

And her health? Kendall sleeps well most nights and, if her daughter is not sleeping well, Kendall and her husband take turns looking after her. Her adrenals are healed, and she has energy to do the things that she enjoys in all areas of her life. Kendall's level of anxiety went from a 9-10 to a 1-2 daily (1-10 scale), and has consistently stayed at that lower level. If she slips back into any of her old patterns that cause her to disconnect from herself and fall off the wagon, she catches it much faster and uses her tools to connect with Something Bigger to bring her back into balance mentally, emotionally and physically again.

In Kendall's Own Words:

It has been a mind-blowing experience to see and feel the difference after working with Tanya.

After only two months, my level of anxiety went from extremely high to almost non-existent. I

now feel more present in my body and with the people that I love. I had many different types of support in the past (meditation, therapy, acupuncture, yoga, etc.) to stay in balance, but coaching with Tanya and learning the Therapeutic Meditation Process and 10 Vibrant Body & Abundant Life Blueprint Keys, plus using the guided practices and other tools, feels like the missing link in my healing process.

Tanya's process brings the best aspects of Eastern philosophy and Western psychology together into a super easy-to-use method. The impacts are immediate and deep. On top of that, Tanya's kindness, patience and insight have kept me feeling supported through the entire process. I feel I've gained the skills and tools that will benefit me, my children, and my family for a lifetime!

– Kendall

Conclusion

Progress not perfection. — Tanya Penny

People often ask me "how long will it take for me to fully heal"? My response is that I honestly don't know. That is up to you, your Something Bigger and your healing path. It is different for each of us. I do know this about the healing process:

- Consistency is important. Using the tips and tools in this book daily (as well as the other healing modalities you use) will ensure you heal as much as possible, as fast as possible.

- Believing that it is possible to fully heal will support a positive outcome.

- Trust your healing process. Do not compare yourself to others.

- Aim for progress not perfection. Look for small positive shifts — mentally, physically and emotionally — each day.

- Never listen to anyone who tells you that you can't fully heal.

- There will be ups and downs: expect them. Know you will get through the tough times.

It took me six years to fully heal the MS that had seeded itself in my body. Even though I no longer have the MS or the physical symptoms that went with it, I am still walking the healing path, finding deeper layers of trauma that are calling for attention, love and healing. They come to the surface when they are ready.

I hope this book has provided you hope for fully healing and that using the tools supports your healing journey. Remember to be brave. Keep walking your healing path. Listen to your inner guidance. Surround yourself with those who support your healing.

If you have any questions or would like to receive more support from me to fully heal your illness, trauma or other life breakdown, I would love to have a conversation with you. Email me directly at tanya@tanyapenny.com.

I look forward to connecting with and supporting you too.

Sending you love and courage,

Tanya Penny ☺

About the Author

Tanya Penny is an Occupational Therapist and Vibrant Body & Abundant Life Coach.

For 25 years of her life, she experienced anxiety, depression, pain, and she carried extra weight. In 2004, Tanya was diagnosed with Multiple Sclerosis. That was a wake-up call that indicated there were some deeper issues in need of love, attention, and release — issues that medications, lifestyle changes, and medical interventions couldn't touch.

It wasn't easy (she had to peel back the layers and really look into her Self) and it wasn't quick (it took years), but she healed. She believes there is a place and a time for doctors and Western medicine, but if you are 100% committed to healing all areas of your life, your soul is called to go on a journey as well.

Now, Penny teaches the Therapeutic Meditation Process and the 10 Vibrant Body and Abundant Life Keys, trusting that they will find their way into the hearts and lives of those who need it, and who are ready to take the journey of discovery that lies ahead. Find out more about her work at **www.TanyaPenny.com.**

Manor House
905-648-2193
www.manor-house-publishing.com

CPSIA information can be obtained
at www.ICGtesting.com
Printed in the USA
FSOW03n0431200218
44627FS